THE SECOND MOST IMPORTANT BOOK YOU WILL EVER READ

A personal challenge to read the Bible

THE SECOND MOST IMPORTANT BOOK YOU WILL EVER READ

A personal challenge to read the Bible

Dan Patrick

ROYAL BOOKS

NASHVILLE

A Division of Thomas Nelson, Inc.
www.ThomasNelson.com

Published in Nashville, Tennessee by Thomas Nelson, Inc.

Cover Design: Suzanne W. Crolley, Designs by Suzanne

Library of Congress Cataloging-in-Publication Data

ISBN 0-7852-6286-5

Printed in the United States of America

02 03 04 05 06 BVG 5 4 3 2

DEDICATION

*This book is dedicated to fulfilling God's command
to make disciples of all men:
"Go…and make disciples of all the nations,
baptizing them in the name of the
Father and of the Son and of the Holy Spirit,
teaching them to observe all things
that I have commanded you."
(Matthew 28:19–20)*

*It is also dedicated to the most loving and
supportive family any man could ask for,
of which I am very proud:
Jan, Ryan, and Shane.
They make life worth living!*

ENDORSEMENTS

What people are saying about
The Second Most Important Book You Will Ever Read:

"Dan's book is a highly readable but insightful look at practical Christianity. You will come away with renewed interest and enthusiasm. Don't pick up this book unless you plan to read it—once you begin, you won't put it down!"
—DR. ED YOUNG
SENIOR PASTOR, SECOND BAPTIST CHURCH, HOUSTON, TEXAS

"I encourage you to read this book. Dan Patrick brings alive the power and promise of the Bible…this is a book that will literally save your life."
—PETER BRADLEY
PRESIDENT, INTERNATIONAL BIBLE SOCIETY

"This book is a wonderfully told and easily read account of Dan's journey to a place in life where he wants us all to be. With this book he hopes to shorten your journey."
—APOLLO 7 ASTRONAUT WALTER CUNNINGHAM
COLONEL, U.S.M.C.

"Dan has written, with clarity and conviction, a book that is destined to introduce God's Word to a new generation, while reinvigorating the faith in the rest of us. At a time when so many are rushing to understand Islam, Dan's book is a much-needed reminder that all the answers we need are in the Bible."
—LAURA INGRAHAM
AUTHOR OF *THE HILARY TRAP* AND HOST OF "THE LAURA INGRAHAM SHOW"

"You will be challenged, inspired, and encouraged as you turn the pages. Dan Patrick has made an invaluable contribution to us all. I'm already making a list of people I want to buy copies for."
—DR. RICK SCARBOROUGH
FOUNDER, VISION AMERICA

"The Bible is the MOST important book you will ever read. Dan's book will help you begin an exciting journey to discover God's plan for you."
—DR. LARS DUNBERG
FOUNDER AND PRESIDENT, GLOBAL ACTION

ACKNOWLEDGEMENTS

*I want to thank my pastor, Dr. Ed Young,
for helping me truly to understand God's Word. Part of this book
is based on lessons learned through his sermons.*

*I want to thank my friend, Mike Richards,
who is a living example of how a godly person should live
their life on a daily basis.*

*I also want to thank Dr. John Bisagno
for speaking to my heart twenty-three years ago, starting
me on the path to following God's Word, not just on Sundays
but every day.*

*These three men, along with many other
Christian friends, have been a source of inspiration to live a life
dedicated to Christ. Their collective stories, thoughts, and
conversations helped build a foundation for this book.*

CONTENTS

SECTION 3

Dan's Top Ten Benefits of Bible Reading

SECTION 4

Getting Started

Points of Interest

WHY READ THIS BOOK?

Why should you read this book? It's a legitimate question.

Who is Dan Patrick and why should you read what he has to say? Another legitimate question.

Why is Dan Patrick so fired up about what he has to say in this book?

I'm so glad you asked! Here are the answers....

THE SECOND MOST IMPORTANT BOOK YOU'LL EVER READ

D id you buy this book?

Did someone loan or give you a copy?

Maybe you are just browsing through it because you were intrigued by the title.

Whatever your reason, it is not an accident. I believe God wanted you reading this page at this moment. "Surely the LORD is in this place, and I did not know it." (Gen. 28:16)

I want to tell you right up front why I titled this book *The SECOND Most Important Book You'll Ever Read*. The reason is very simple. I want you to read THE MOST IMPORTANT book ever written, the Holy Bible. I want to inspire you, encourage you, admonish you, and even "intrigue" you into reading the Bible.

Why?

Although according to a recent poll, almost every American owns or has access to a Bible, only twelve percent of Americans have read the entire Bible. Only twenty-two percent of Americans have read part of the New Testament. Many people know a few popular Bible stories, but beyond that, know very little about what is in the Bible. Therefore, if my book leads you to read the Bible, then indeed my book will live up to its title.

I also know that as you read the Bible, your life is going to change in ways too numerous to count or too grand to imagine.

If you have little or no faith in God, it may be that you have never taken the time to read the Bible. This book is for you.

If you attend church, but still don't know or read the Bible, this book is for you.

And if you are a Christian who is a student of the Bible, this book will reinforce your faith and give you sound arguments in simple terms to share with unbelievers. In fact, I encourage you to buy additional copies to give to your family members and friends who don't know Jesus Christ. In doing so, you will fulfill God's greatest commandment—to share the Gospel with all the world.

What motivated me to write this book?

I regularly meet people—both those in church and those who rarely, if ever, go to church—who admit to me that they don't read their Bibles. Some don't read the Bible because they don't believe they can understand what they read. In fact, some believe the Bible can only be read and understood by Christian leaders, such as pastors and priests. Others don't read because they don't believe the Bible is relevant for today, or more specifically, for their personal lives today. Still others don't read because they question the factual accuracy of various parts of the Bible. Some don't read simply because they don't want to give up a life of guilt-free living. And others see no reason to read the Bible because they think they already know right from wrong.

I understand all of these arguments. In fact, I once held to a couple of them myself. But...I also disagree with each of these premises. In the second section of this book, I'm going to take on those excuses. If you hold to one of these opinions, I challenge you to read what I have to say with an open heart and mind.

I believe the Bible CAN be read and understood by *everyone*.

I believe the Bible IS highly relevant for every issue you face in your life, or will face. It is also relevant for every problem your loved ones and friends are encountering, or will encounter.

I believe the Bible can be trusted as being absolutely one hundred percent true.

And I believe the Bible is our key to experiencing a better world, beginning with a better personal life for every individual. It's far more than a book of rules or an explanation of right and wrong. It's a key to feeling loved, becoming a loving person, finding peace, and experiencing true happiness in life.

Finally, I believe God expects ALL people to read the Bible for themselves so that He might speak directly to their hearts and minds, and give them guidance that is very practical, highly personal, always applicable, and never wrong.

So Who Made Me an Expert?

You may be asking, "So what makes Dan Patrick an expert on this? What qualifies Dan to be the author of this book?"

I do not profess to be a Bible scholar or expert. Far from it. I am not one of those people who can quote chapter and verse on every topic. I'm a person of average ability and intelligence. And I know this…if I can understand God's message, anyone can. If reading the Bible can change me, reading the Bible can change any person. If the Bible is relevant to my ordinary, occasionally extraordinary, and sometimes sub-par life, then the Bible is relevant to your life, too!

For the past several years, the main focus of my life has been to learn more about what the Bible has to say to me. This doesn't mean I'm a man without hobbies or other interests. I still enjoy traveling, watching movies, playing my guitar, and driving old cars. And above all, I enjoy spending as much time as possible with my wife and two children.

The *foremost* interest of my life, however, has become the Bible. I watch and listen to tapes about the Bible whenever possible. I read the Bible and books written about the Bible every chance I get. Every time I learn something new, even from chapters and verses I have read many times, I feel an exhilaration in my soul that can't be matched. The Bible is exciting! If you don't think so, you haven't read it very much lately. The Bible is as relevant as today's news headlines. Maybe even more relevant!

In fact, I would rather sit down and reread parts of the Bible that I enjoy than read the latest *New York Times* bestseller. I find that the Bible has everything any book could offer. It has intrigue … mystery … action … drama … heroism … sex … tender love … treachery … betrayal … restoration … comedy … and more self-help tips than an entire bookstore can dish up.

There isn't a problem in life that doesn't have an answer in the Bible. Indeed, I am firmly convinced that if more people went to the Bible first for *answers* to their questions and problems, there not only would be far fewer problems, but there would be far less need for counselors, divorce attorneys, courts of law, and therapists.

TAKING THE CHALLENGE

What about you?

Have you read the entire Bible?

Have you read the entire New Testament?

Have you read at least parts of the Old Testament and parts of the New Testament?

Do you know the difference between the Old Testament and New Testament?

If your answer to any of the above questions is "no," I can relate. They were my answers, too. Twenty years ago, I owned a Bible. I just didn't read it.

And if *you* aren't reading the Bible, you don't know what you are missing.

As mentioned, I'm going to address why *you* and others don't read the Bible. But before we begin, I want to share two of the most amazing stories I have ever heard about God's power to change hearts. These stories were told directly to me by the people involved. I believe that after reading these two stories you will be inspired to read the rest of this book...and then the Bible...to discover what God has to say about your life!

DOES THE BIBLE'S MESSAGE REALLY WORK? AMAZING STORIES!

Over the years I have met a number of people who have shared with me amazing stories about how God's Word has changed their lives. These people have come from many walks of life. Their stories have shown me that there isn't any person, in any place, who doesn't need God in their life, and there isn't anyone who is beyond being touched by God—no matter who they are, where they are, what they have, or what they've done.

I want to share just two of these stories with you. These are stories of people I have interviewed and I truly believe you will find their stories amazing. If I was titling these stories as a book, I would describe them this way:

From the Lights of Hollywood to
the Darkness of the Jungle—
Amazing Stories of Amazing Grace

I hope these two stories will reinforce to you the MAIN POINT OF THE BIBLE: You need God in your life, and no matter who you are or the guilt you are carrying, God loves you and will forgive you.

A Story of Restored Love and Marriage

If you have ever watched *The Mary Tyler Moore Show* or *The Love Boat* on television, you have seen Gavin MacLeod. He played the part of a writer named Murray Slaughter on *The Mary Tyler Moore Show*. Then he went on to star as Captain Stubing on *The Love Boat*.

One day I saw Gavin and his wife, Patti, on the Trinity Broadcasting Network, a Christian television network. As I heard Gavin and Patti share their faith and love for the Lord, I wanted to know more about them. I set up an interview to promote a stage show that Gavin was doing in Houston. We talked briefly about the show and then I asked him if he would mind sharing his faith with the audience. He seemed shocked that someone in the secular media would be interested, but he was more than happy to share his story—it was a story I found truly inspiring.

Gavin told me and my audience that he was not a Christian when he was acting on the television shows I mentioned above. He told that he had always been very impressed with Mary Tyler Moore and that he knew it was up to the "star" of a show to make sure the show was successful—many jobs and careers depended on how a show's star worked. Therefore, when he got his own chance to star in *The Love Boat*, he took the role very seriously and became consumed with the responsibility he felt toward the cast and crew and to his new "star" status. He worked twelve to fifteen hours a day. His wife of many years, Patti, complained that he was working too hard and spending too much time away from home. He told her that he didn't have time for her, and that his show was more important than their marriage. They divorced.

Several years later, with *The Love Boat* a big hit, Gavin's mother became very ill. Although he was not a Christian at the time, he prayed that God would spare his mother's life and he promised God he would do anything God asked of him if only God would heal her.

During this time, Patti visited the hospital. She and Gavin had not had much contact with each other for several years. He had heard that Patti had become a Christian but he didn't know much more about her. She suggested that he come over for dinner and he accepted her invitation. Over dinner, Patti told Gavin how she had become a Christian and had joined a group of divorced Christian women who were praying for their former husbands to return to them. As part of their faith walk, these women had a practice of saying aloud as they returned home each evening, "Hi, honey, I'm home!" They prayed daily that their husbands would one day return to them and be able to answer their greeting.

Gavin's mother recovered, and his love for Patti rekindled. He told me how impressed he was with his former wife's faith and her new outlook on life. He started watching evangelical preachers on television and spending more time with Patti. In time, Gavin accepted Jesus as his Savior and he and Patti remarried.

The next part of his story choked him up as he shared it with me. And every time I retell this part of the story, I get choked up, too! Shortly after Gavin and Patti remarried, his wife came home one day and called out, "Hi, honey, I'm home." Gavin, remembering how she had once told him of this ritual of faith when she was alone, answered back, "Honey, I'm here." He was overcome with tears of joy as he spoke those words to her. God, indeed, had been faithful to both of them.

As I heard Gavin tell this story, I couldn't help but think, Here was a man who seemingly had it all to the outside world, but in reality, he was empty inside. He was a broken man who knew he needed God in his life but didn't know how to find Him. In truth, Gavin didn't have to find God. God found *him* and used extraordinary circumstances to show Gavin the way to Himself.

Are you like Gavin? Do people *think* you have it made from your outside appearances or behavior? Or maybe you are like Patti, turning your life's heartbreaks and pain over to God, believing through faith that He will answer your prayers? God stands ready to meet you *wherever* you are in your life!

Gavin's story didn't end there. He next told me about the actor Ted Knight, who had played the wacky anchorman Ted Baxter on *The Mary Tyler Moore Show*. Ted had been a serious actor for most of his career, including roles in a number of Shakespeare's plays. Although Ted was a huge hit on Mary's show, he was always saddened a bit that the audience viewed him as a buffoon. He feared his days of serious acting were over. According to Gavin, Ted still wanted to be taken as a serious actor, not perceived to be a clown.

Gavin related how Ted never received the dramatic roles he desired after Mary's show, but Ted did eventually land a starring role in his own comedy television show. The program was a big hit financially and Ted had all the trappings of a star, including the big home in the Hollywood area that he had always wanted. Gavin also told me that off camera, he had always had the highest respect for Ted and they were best friends, even though Gavin's character on the program always seemed to hold the Ted Baxter character in disdain.

Over the years, Gavin and Ted didn't see much of each other because their careers had gone in different directions. Then one day

Gavin received a call from Ted's wife asking him to come over for a visit. Gavin had heard that Ted was ill with cancer, but he had no idea how sick Ted really was. Gavin and Patti were about to leave Los Angeles to go on the road with a stage show, but they decided to visit Ted before they left town.

When they arrived at Ted's home, Ted's wife told them Ted was too sick to come downstairs. Gavin and Patti went up to his room. What Gavin saw next was shocking to him. Ted, once a strapping stocky man of Polish descent, was wasting away in his bed, dying of cancer. Ted could hardly speak, but was glad to see his old friend. He noted that something about Gavin and Patti seemed "special" and he asked what it was that had brought them back together and had given Gavin a new outlook on life. At that point, Gavin shared the Gospel of Jesus Christ with Ted.

Like many people, Ted believed in God, but he did not have a personal relationship with Jesus. He had little understanding of salvation and God's plan for him. After Gavin had shared, Ted crawled out of bed and knelt on the bedroom floor of his Hollywood mansion and accepted Jesus as his Savior. Gavin and Patti left knowing that this would be the last time they saw Ted on earth.

Several weeks later, while touring, Gavin received word that Ted had died. Gavin told me that of all the accolades and accomplishments of his life, nothing would ever mean more to him, or be more important to him, than knowing he had led his dear friend to the Lord and to eternal salvation before it was too late.

Do you know people who need the Lord's salvation before it is too late for them? Do *you* need His salvation?

I was riveted to every word Gavin shared with me and my audience that day. I found his testimony to be powerful as it pointed to the awesome love, grace, and promises of God's Word. Over the years since that day, I have seen Gavin and Patti share other words of encouragement on the Trinity Broadcasting Network—they speak in a profound way to those who are in troubled relationships and marriages. Gavin and Patti have set aside what many in our world would say is important in life—namely, money, fame, and power—to share their story about what really brings peace in life, the Word of God.

From the glitz of Hollywood and the story of people who had everything in life, let me now take you to one of the darkest, most remote places in the world where people have very little in the way of material goods, need God in their lives just as much as those who are wealthy, and who are *loved* by God just as much as peoples in more civilized parts of the world.

A STORY OF THE POWER OF GENUINE FORGIVENESS

Have you ever asked yourself the question many people ask about God's ability to have His Word heard by people in the jungles of the world? Some people use this question as their excuse for not believing in God. Well, if you thought the last story was an amazing testimony to the power of God to change lives, let me say as they used to say in vaudeville acts, "You ain't heard nothin' yet!"

I don't know if I would have believed the following story if the person who was directly involved had not personally told me his story. Believe me, his story is true! Without question, it is one of the most amazing stories I have ever heard about how God can change the human heart and bring about real forgiveness.

In late 1955, a major oil company had a plan for drilling for oil in a remote jungle area in Ecuador. There was a serious problem, however.

Several tribes in the area had killed every outsider who ventured into their territory. In fact, these tribes were so brutal they were known as some of the most murderous tribes ever studied by anthropologists.

The government of Ecuador wanted the company to drill in their nation, but the oil executives said that unless this problem was resolved, they would go elsewhere. Several missionaries feared the government, in an effort to comply with the company's ultimatum, would wipe out the tribes before the Gospel could be presented to them. These missionaries decided to go to the jungle in an attempt to bring them the Word of God. They were hoping these tribesmen could be reached with the Gospel, which they believed would also bring a peaceful solution to the standoff.

The missionaries, one of whom was a pilot, flew over the jungle area for days dropping gifts to the people below. Then, they found a landing area and decided it was time to make personal contact with the tribal people.

The first day several tribesmen and women came out to see and touch these strange visitors who had come out of the sky. A major language barrier prevented significant communication, but the three men hoped that their peaceful actions would send a message that they were not in the area to harm any members of the tribe.

A few days later, on January 8, 1956, four native women came out of the jungle. While they were distracting the missionaries, several men came out of the jungle and speared the missionaries to death.

Many years later one of these tribesmen told a translator that they had been curious as to why one of the missionaries had seemed to run to the plane to get something to eat even as he was being speared to death. What had actually happened was that this man had run to the cockpit of their small plane to grab the radio microphone to call for help. The natives did not know what a microphone was, and they thought he was trying to eat some type of food before he died. These tribal people were not connected to the modern world in any way.

Determined not to let these tribal people die without the Gospel, the sister and a friend of two of the missionaries went back to the jungle to try to bring the Word of God to the killers of their family members. One of the slain missionaries had a baby boy and wife who were living just on the edge of the jungle. The baby's aunt, whose brother had been killed, convinced her sister-in-law to let her take this baby to the jungle to be raised. The mother agreed.

Over many years, the aunt became known as "Star" to the tribal people. She slowly learned their language and brought the Word of God to the people. Many of them accepted Jesus as their Savior.

A few years ago I met the boy who grew up in the jungle. His name is Steve Saint. I realize that may sound like a made-up-in-Hollywood name to you but it truly is his real name. The people he grew up with in the jungle were the people who killed his father, Nate Saint.

Steve brought along a tribal leader with him to our interview session. This man's name was Mincaye (pronounced Min-ky-e) of the Waodan Tribe. Mincaye appeared to be about seventy years old. Through Steve's translation, Mincaye told me and my television audience how he and his tribe had lived very "badly-badly." He said that Star, Steve's aunt, had taught them about Jesus and the Holy Spirit and that he had learned that if he lived badly-badly, he would suffer for his actions. He had a poison-tipped dart with him and laid it on my news desk. It was black. He explained that once his heart was as dark as the dart, but that after he learned about Jesus and the Holy Spirit, his heart was now clean like a sky with no clouds.

One more thing that is vital for you to know—Mincaye is the man who killed Steve's father. He was a young warrior at the time and he knew no other way of life. Steve grew up knowing Mincaye had killed his father. Yet today, Steve calls Mincaye "grandfather" to his own children. He is like a son to Mincaye.

I said to Steve that I thought his actions were the most stunning act of human forgiveness I had ever encountered. He disagreed and said that it was Mincaye who had forgiven *him*. I didn't understand. Steve then explained that according to tribal laws, Steve was *expected* to avenge the death of his father once he was an adult. He was *expected* to kill Mincaye. Mincaye knew this, and therefore, he *should* have killed Steve while Steve was still a child. He certainly had countless opportunities to do so. But according to Steve Saint, after Mincaye received Jesus as his Savior, Mincaye forgave the "future intentions" of Steve and instead of killing Steve, raised him like a son. Steve told me that this was the ultimate act of forgiveness in their story.

In our interview session, Steve quoted a verse from Revelation that he said was the reason for his father's original mission, and the reason for his own missionary work today: "You were slain, and have redeemed us to God by Your blood out of every tribe and tongue and people and nation, and have made us kings and priests to our God; and we shall reign on the earth." (Rev. 5:9)

Today, Steve and Mincaye travel the world telling their story. A movie about their experience is being planned.

These two stories—the first about Gavin and Patti MacLeod and Ted Baxter, and the second about Steve Saint and Mincaye of the Waodan Tribe—are real-life testimonies about the power of God and His ability to change hearts. God can reach the rich and famous who may have pushed God away. God can reach the unknown souls of this earth who have never even heard His name.

The good news is that Gavin, Patti, Ted, Steve, and Mincaye all accepted the Bible's teachings and in turn, Jesus as their Savior. There are those, however, who read and hear and still reject the Bible. Don't be one of them!

No person can transform his or her own heart. It simply isn't possible, because only a *sinless* sacrifice can atone for a *sinful* person. Forgiveness of sin is God's work. It is a transforming work that not only changes the human heart, but human behavior.

I have told these stories to people and had them respond, "But I don't understand." The fact is, you can't fully understand how these stories can be true unless you read God's words and believe them. Once you begin reading the Bible, you will see events such as these, and even see experiences in your own life, in a way you have never seen them before.

The next time someone tells you that a person doesn't need the Bible if he or she has a great career and material success in life...tell them about Gavin and Patti and Ted. The next time someone argues with you that God doesn't care about native peoples in the most remote areas of the world, tell them about Mincaye and Steve Saint.

Let me ask you today: Is your heart as dark as a poison dart? Have you lived badly-badly? Have you put the things of this world ahead of the things of God? You can live with the same confidence and peace that millions of Christians experience on a day-to-day basis, even in circumstances that are painful, sorrowful, or impoverished.

Don't take my word for it. Take God's Word for it! The Bible says that you, too, can have a clean heart like a sky with no clouds!

My Replies to the Four Biggest Excuses

I told you that the two stories in the last chapter were an amazing testament to God's power to change hearts and lives in believers and nonbelievers alike. Now, let's focus on four of the most common reasons people (maybe you) give for not reading the Bible.

EXCUSE #1

"But Dan...The Bible Is Too Hard to Understand"

"The Bible is just too hard to understand."

That, without a doubt, is the most common excuse I hear for people NOT reading the Bible.

Do you think the Bible is a book with hundreds of people and places that have names too difficult to pronounce, stories that defy logical explanation, and hard-to-comprehend images?

Do you think the Bible can only be understood by spiritual leaders, such as pastors or priests? Do you think God intended for only a FEW people to be able to understand His Word?

My answer to each of these questions is, "NO!" God WANTS to communicate with ALL men and women. He WANTS us to understand His Word. He's made it very easy in the twenty-first century for us to do so.

I Once Used this Excuse

For most of my life, I stayed away from reading the Bible. I thought it was too complex and confusing. Every time I started reading it at the beginning, I'd get about a hundred or so pages in and find myself bored to tears.

I also was intimidated by people who seemed to know a great deal more about Bible people, places, and subjects than I knew. I was very uncomfortable about people who would say such things as, "Dan, do you remember what the Bible said about…?" Or "Dan, isn't this circumstance just like the one in the Bible about…?" I'd just nod and try to change the subject. I could never figure out if they really thought I knew and were testing me, or were just trying to show off their knowledge of the Bible.

And then I started reading the Bible for myself and made some amazing discoveries about things nobody had told me about!

You've Got to Know How to Find the Good Stuff!

Let me clue you into a couple of things. First, the best way to read the Bible is NOT from cover to cover. If you read the Bible straight through as if you are reading a novel, you'll probably get about as far as a few chapters into Leviticus (the third book in the Bible) and quit!

The Bible is actually sixty-six books in one. Some of those books are a whole lot more interesting and easier to read than others. Leviticus is one of the most difficult, least interesting, and in my opinion, most boring—at least until you've read everything else a few times!

My personal recommendation is that you read the books of Matthew and John first. In fact, I suggest you read these two books several times or until you have a good feel for their message. Each time you read them through, you'll learn something new. I also suggest that you start reading in Matthew at chapter 1, verse 17.

I love reading the Sermon on the Mount, which is a compilation of what Jesus taught in a number of different settings at different times. Like many preachers, Jesus tended to preach the same message over and over to different groups of people. The Sermon on the Mount is Matthew's account of these frequently-taught messages put together into one sermon. It can be found in Matthew chapters 5–7.

The first few verses of the Sermon on the Mount are called the "beatitudes"—the word literally means the "blessing statements."

The books of Matthew and John will give you all of the basic information you need to know to accept Jesus as your Savior and to begin to follow and apply His teachings to live a life of fulfillment, peace, and true happiness.

Then read Luke and Acts—they go together as almost one book. Then read Romans, Mark, Proverbs, Genesis, and Exodus.

Once you have read these books, begin to explore!

SOME VERSIONS ARE EASIER TO READ THAN OTHERS

Let me also clue you into the fact that not all versions of the Bible are the same. For years—even centuries—the King James Version of the Bible was just about the only version widely available. That version is written in language filled with Thees and Thous and Thines. That's hardly the way we speak today!

The Bible references in this book are from the New King James Version of the Bible. This version is easy-to-read and written in easy-to-understand English. There are other fine versions or translations that are also easy to read in modern English—among them are the New International Version, the New American Standard Version, and the New Revised Standard Version.

I like books that are easy to read and quick to the point. I do NOT like to read books that are written in jargon or language I can't readily understand.

Let's try out a little of the New King James Version to see if you can understand what it says:

- "Do not fret because of evildoers,
  Nor be envious of the workers of iniquity.
  For they shall soon be cut down like the grass,
  And wither as the green herb." (Ps. 37:1-2)

- "Delight yourself also in the LORD,
  And He shall give you the desires of your heart." (Ps. 37:4)

- "Listen to counsel and receive instruction,
  That you may be wise in your latter days." (Prov. 19:20)

- "Jesus, walking by the Sea of Galilee, saw two brothers, Simon called Peter, and Andrew his brother, casting a net into the sea; for they were fishermen. And He said to them, 'Follow Me, and I will make you fishers of men.' Then they immediately left their nets and followed Him." (Matt. 4:18–20)

- Jesus said: "When you do a charitable deed, do not sound a trumpet before you as the hypocrites do in the synagogues and in the streets, that they may have glory from men.

Assuredly, I say to you, they have their reward. But when you do a charitable deed, do not let your left hand know what your right hand is doing, that your charitable deed may be in secret; and your Father who sees in secret will Himself reward you openly." (Matt. 6:2–4)

- "Let love be without hypocrisy. Abhor what is evil. Cling to what is good. Be kindly affectionate to one another with brotherly love, in honor giving preference to one another; not lagging in diligence, fervent in spirit, serving the Lord; rejoicing in hope, patient in tribulation, continuing steadfastly in prayer; distributing to the needs of the saints, given to hospitality." (Rom. 12:9–13)

There—you have just read six passages from the Bible. You've read parts from the Old Testament and New Testament. And I have no doubt that you *understood* every one of the fifteen verses you just read. There are thousands more just like them.

Plain and simple, you *can* understand the Bible.

CHOOSING THE RIGHT BIBLE FOR YOU

Now, if you don't own an easy-to-read Bible, get one. Go to a Bible bookstore and browse. Choose a Bible that *you* like.

Here's a simple way to test-drive a Bible version: Open the book at about the half-way point. You'll probably be in the Psalms. Read a couple of paragraphs. Then turn over to about three-quarters the way through. You'll be somewhere in the New Testament. Read a couple of paragraphs there.

Do you see red letters in the version you pick up? Those are the statements attributed to Jesus. I recommend a Bible that has His words in red letters—it makes it easier to sift out what Jesus said from what others around Him said. Bibles that have this feature are usually labeled "Red Letter Edition."

Bibles also come in different styles and sizes of typeface. Pick a size that's easy for you to read without eye strain.

Take a look at the "extras" the Bible might have. Lots of Bibles today have special study notes, maps, charts, and so forth. Some have an index or concordance that gives a listing of various topics and verses related to them—which can be of great help in finding answers to specific questions or solutions to specific problems. Some Bibles have devotional insights into various passages—little essays that help interpret a passage or give added insight into what God is saying.

Here are some of the helps that are found in many editions of the Bible:

- **Pronunciation Help**. Some Bibles give "pronunciation" helps for Bible names of people and places. Such a Bible can be very valuable to a person who is teaching the Bible or who is regularly called upon to read the Bible in public.

- **Cross References**. Many Bibles give related references—for example, the Old Testament reference for a verse that may be quoted in the New Testament. Sometimes these cross references are in a center column between text columns, sometimes they are at the bottom of a page. Some Bibles also provide references that are related to the same *topic* being addressed by a Bible passage.

- **Insights and Study Helps**. Many Bibles today give added information that provides insights into the meaning of certain Bible words, concepts, principles, customs, or teachings. The vast majority of Bibles have information at the beginning of each book that tells more about the author, setting, and content of the book. Some include an outline of the book, a reading plan for the book, or highlights of key concepts covered in the book.

- **Indices, Maps, Charts, and Other "Helps."** Go to the back of the Bible you are examining. See what's there! Some Bibles have commentary on various sections of the Bible, others have maps, charts, an index of key Bible concepts, and so forth.

Paperback or leather? The choice is up to you! IMPORTANT: Don't buy a Bible that is so expensive you are going to be reluctant to pick it up, scribble notes in it, or take it with you in your car or out to the sands of the beach. Buy one that you are most likely to read and mark up with your own notes, questions, insights, or dates. By the way, why not grab a pen and make notes in *this* book, too!

Finally, you may just want to consider starting with a children's Bible—one with lots of illustrations. I'm serious. Don't be embarrassed. The language is very simple. You can explore the Bible even as you read it to your children! Even if you don't have children, this can be a good start. It's a great way to become familiar with some of the major stories and people of the Bible. This approach was one I used in my early days of Bible reading.

YOU GOTTA MAKE TIME FOR GOD'S WORD

"Too hard to understand" is the *excuse* given, but I don't think it's the real reason people don't read the Bible. The truth is, most people think the Bible is "too hard to understand in a *brief amount of time*." Many people simply don't open their Bible because they believe they are too busy to fit Bible-reading into their more-important schedules.

I suggest that you have a small, easy-to-read Bible that you can take with you when you travel. You might even want to keep it in your car or briefcase. All of us in today's world seem to have little pockets of fifteen minutes here and there when we are waiting for a plane or riding a bus or find ourselves sitting in a waiting room with outdated magazines. Use those times to read your Bible.

The Five and Ten Plan

I like to recommend that people read the Bible in five and ten-minute bursts. Given my background in radio, I know that ten minutes is about the length of a couple of calls and a couple of commercials. Surely God's Word is worthy of that much time in a day!

A Daily Habit

No person would willingly choose to go an entire day without food (unless the person was intentionally abstaining from food for some reason). What makes us think we can go an entire day without some spiritual food? We need nourishment from God's Word on a daily basis just as much as we need nutritious food on a daily basis. That's why God's Word is called the "bread of life." Jesus said in the New Testament, quoting a verse from the Old Testament, "Man shall not live by bread alone, but by every word that proceeds from the mouth of God." (Matt. 4:4 and Deut. 8:3)

Read until you feel "full." At times, that might mean reading longer. Read until you receive some new idea or concept to mull over or "chew on" in your mind. Read until you can say to yourself,

"Hmmm. That's something worth thinking about" or, "That's really true for me right now."

Finding a quiet time every day to read your Bible can, and should, become a habit that's just as "automatic" to you as eating or brushing your teeth.

Reading Plans

There are a number of books that tell you how to read the Bible in a year. There are even Bibles that are structured so you can read a portion each day and get through the Bible in a year. These may be helpful to you. I find, however, that many people get bogged down in certain parts of the Old Testament and become discouraged. If the read-through-the-Bible-in-a-year approach doesn't work for you, I suggest you find certain stories or books of the Bible and read those first. Get a good sense of the "whole" of the Bible—even if you have read portions of it many times. Look for common themes and recurring principles.

MORE CLUES ABOUT THE BIBLE'S STRUCTURE

Some people seem to think they can't understand HOW to find things in the Bible. They don't understand the "structure" of the Bible. Let me give you a couple more vital clues.

The Bible books are broken into chapters and verses for easier reference. Many Bibles have "subheadings" associated with chapters or portions of chapters that can help you get straight to a section that you want. In a Bible reference, the name of the book is given first, followed by the chapter, and then the verse. For example: Genesis 12:1 refers to the book of Genesis, the twelfth chapter, and the first verse.

Throughout this book, Bible books will be abbreviated when references are given after a quoted passage. The abbreviations can be found in Section 4.

WATCH OUT—YOU MIGHT START LIKING THIS!

I have absolutely no doubt that once you begin spending time in the Word of God, you *will want* to read it more and learn more from it. My job is to get you started. I take very seriously the command that Jesus gave to His close followers nearly two thousand years ago, "Go therefore and make disciples of all the nations, baptizing them in the name of the Father and of the Son and of the Holy Spirit, teaching them to observe all things that I have commanded you; and lo, I am with you always, even to the end of the age." (Matt. 28:19–20)

In order to do what Jesus commanded, you have to know what He said. In order to know what He said, you have to read the Bible. In fact, how can a person argue against the Word of God if they haven't taken the time to read it?

The truth is, most people who reject God, or do not live in a godly manner, haven't read the Bible.

4

EXCUSE #2

"But Dan…The Bible Isn't Relevant for Today's World"

"That was then. This is now. Surely you don't think the Bible is applicable to *today's* world." Is that your excuse? If so, consider these headlines:

- LEADER GETS CAUGHT IN AFFAIR
- CLOSE ASSOCIATE OF LEADER TURNS TRAITOR
- SON DISAPPEARS; FATHER FEARS MURDER
- THREE NATIONS ATTACK JERUSALEM
- WOMAN SEEKS JUSTICE AFTER SONS ARE KILLED
- SHIP CRASHES AGAINST ROCKS BUT ALL ARE SAFE

Each of the above headlines could easily have appeared in today's morning newspaper.

Consider these storylines:

- Woman buys property in hopes of helping husband.

- Mother uses ingenious ploy to save infant from death.

- Father refuses to face rape of daughter.

- Military leader sends spies into enemy territory.

- Sister criticizes brother for marriage to foreign woman.

These "plots" could easily be on today's soap-opera and prime-time television programs.

All of these headlines and storylines are in the Bible!

Those who claim the Bible isn't for today usually hold to a position that the world has changed since Bible times. Well, technology and political entities may have changed since then…but human nature hasn't changed a bit! Men and women today are just as jealous … treacherous … ambitious … vengeful … greedy … lustful … rebellious … power-hungry … angry … hateful … and prejudiced today as they were thousands of years ago.

When people say the Bible isn't for today, what they usually *mean* is they don't think the Bible is for THEIR personal life today. Actually, most people who use this excuse for not reading the Bible don't WANT the Bible to be applicable to their personal life. They fear the Bible just might call them to change some things they don't want to change! Mark Twain once said, "It's not the things I don't understand about the Bible that bother me; it's the things I do understand that bother me."

I once used this excuse and I admit that I was a little afraid about what the Bible might say about my life. I feared I might have to stop doing some of the things I liked to do. One of my main impressions of the Bible was that it was a book filled with the phrase, "thou shalt not." Of course, all of those "thou shalt nots" were related, in my mind at least, to things that I *wanted* to do. Living a thou-shalt-not life didn't sound like much fun.

I believed in some type of God. I just wasn't sure about the God of the Bible.

MY SLOW CRAWL TOWARD THE TRUTH

Let me tell you a little about how I came to recognize that the Bible was relevant to my life. The fact is, I didn't seek out God as much as He sought me. I believe that's true for every person. God is continually going after us, desiring to have a relationship with us and desiring to communicate with us.

I grew up in a blue-collar neighborhood in Baltimore, Maryland, in the 1950s. I was an only child. My grandfather on my dad's side was a dedicated Catholic. I remember him going to mass almost every night. He died of cancer and it took my father a long time to forgive God for "taking" my grandfather home to heaven. My mother came from Virginia and had no particular religious roots that I recall.

When I was old enough to attend Sunday school on my own, my parents made sure I attended. For a while we attended a Lutheran church as a family but that didn't last long. Today, both of my parents are Christians. My mother attends church on a regular basis and her faith is an important part of her life. My dad prays on a daily basis and has embraced Jesus as his Savior.

Looking back on my childhood, knowing what I know now, I know we were NOT a Christian family at that time. I am grateful my parents taught me right from wrong and that they were "good" people and good parents. But we weren't Christians.

As I became a teenager, I rarely had a thought about God. Every night I recited the familiar prayer, "Now I lay me down to sleep"…but I did so by rote as a habit. Occasionally I'd pray to ask God to help me make the team, win the game, get me a date, or help me pass a test. But overall, I was clueless when it came to prayer. I was also clueless about the Bible. I believed that Jesus lived, and I would probably even have told you that I believed He was the Son of God, but I had no idea what His life or death meant to *me*. I couldn't have told you anything Jesus said.

One thing I *did* know deep inside was that I needed to know more about God. I knew I was missing out on something that was important, something bigger than myself. Even so, I didn't care to take the time or make the effort to find out what that "something" might be. I was too busy having fun and living my life according to "Dan's Plan."

The Best Cruise I Never Took

When I was in my twenties, my parents decided to take a cruise. I drove them to the dock so they could board the ship, and I waited on the dock for my grandparents to arrive—they were coming to say "Bon voyage." I wasn't going on the cruise. I was just there to make sure everything went well in their debarkation.

While I was waiting on the dock, a car pulled up and the driver asked me for directions about where to park. It was apparent the driver thought I worked for the cruise line. I noticed that a beautiful blonde woman was seated in the passenger side of the front seat.

Later, when I was on board with my grandparents and parents, guess who should come out of the cabin directly across from the one booked by my parents? The blonde! As it turned out, her mom was taking the cruise and she was only there to make sure all went well with her mother's trip. All of those decks ... and all of those cabins...and there she was across from my parents' cabin. A coincidence? Someone once told me that coincidences are God's way of staying anonymous. I agree. A very popular movie starring Mel Gibson, *Signs*, has a theme dealing with the concept of coincidence. If you haven't seen it, it's a terrific flick (albeit a little scary). I recommend it.

Eight months later, the blonde—Jan Rankin—and I were married. As I write this book, we have just celebrated our twenty-seventh wedding anniversary.

Several months before Jan and I met, Jan's father was killed in an automobile accident. She was twenty-three years old at the time. She had a sister three years younger, and an eight-year-old brother. Although I never met her father, I know he must have been a terrific man. He had worked his way through law school, taking night classes, and had held a high position at the Pentagon. After many years of hard effort, he was just on the verge of truly enjoying the fruits of his labor ... and then he was killed.

Jan's family was Catholic. I marveled at how they all had handled this terrible tragedy. I saw how their faith in God had pulled them through. I knew with a deep knowing that I wanted to have God in my life. My problem was that I didn't know how to go about establishing a connection with God. After all, why would God want a relationship with me after I had ignored Him for so many years?

DREAMING WITH AL ROKER

At the time I met Jan I was a twenty-five-year-old high-school-ring salesman with a company called Herff Jones. I got a promotion to sales manager in Atlanta just before we married. A year later I was transferred by the company to Scranton, Pennsylvania. During our years in Pennsylvania, I attended a Catholic church with Jan. I must confess that I didn't pay much attention to what was going on in church. I was a church daydreamer.

Before Jan and I met, I had attended the University of Maryland (Baltimore County campus). I graduated with a Bachelor of Arts degree in English. I worked full-time while I was in college selling radio advertising time and as a disc jockey for a country music station outside of Baltimore. My goal was to be on television. I dreamed of hosting a game show, or perhaps *The Tonight Show* one day. After I graduated, however, I couldn't get an on-air job in the broadcast industry so I went into sales. I didn't give up my dream. I just put it on a shelf.

One Sunday while in church in Scranton, I prayed and asked God to give me a chance to pursue my dream. I knew it would take a miracle. I had been out of college for almost four years at that point and I felt that if something didn't happen fairly quickly, it wasn't going to happen. I promised God that if He would answer my prayer I would use my position in television as a platform for telling people about Him. Looking back, I realize that I didn't have ANY idea what I would say about Him if given the chance. I also didn't know that it never pays to try to bargain with God. All in all, God probably got a good laugh out of that prayer. I'm sure He has heard just about everything over the last several thousand years. But after He quit laughing, He also seemed to move a mountain that hadn't moved before.

The next day I stopped by the television station located at the Scranton airport. The station was WNEP, an ABC affiliate. It's the station where Bill O'Reilly of *The O'Reilly Factor*, got his start.

I went in cold off the street without an appointment. As it turned out, the station had just fired the weekend weather and sports guy. Another coincidence? As I look back now, I don't believe so.

The news director, a nice man named Eldon Hale, overheard me asking about a job out in the lobby and he invited me into his office. He had also spent some time in radio in Baltimore and despite the fact that I had zero television experience, he gave me an audition. Three days later he hired me part-time on the weekends for the grand sum of $10 for the early news show and $10 for the late news show. That was $5 for giving the weather and $5 for giving the sports news.

What Eldon didn't know is that I would have paid *him* for the chance to have this job. I could hardly believe that I had been given an opportunity for a job in my dream profession just seventy-two hours after I had prayed. *Wow*, I thought, *this prayer stuff really works!*

Seven months later I was hired in Washington, D.C., at WTTG, Channel 5, as the sports director. I had hit the big time in record time. Unbelievable!

Channel 5 was undergoing a youth movement at the time. They hired me and a young weatherman named Al Roker about the same time. The station didn't want to pay high salaries and they knew Al and I were from small markets and we were cheap.

I could tell right away that Al was going places. He was very funny even then. I remember Al sharing with me his dreams about working at the network level some day. Years later when I tuned in *The Today Show* and saw Al there, I felt very happy for him. He was a super guy when I knew him in the seventies and I can only assume he's still a super guy.

GIVE ME THAT OLD-TIME RELIGION

In 1979, I was tired of Washington, D.C. It was a great town to work in as a television anchor. My job got me invited to the White House and to Washington parties. I was able to meet all types of interesting people. But that life wasn't for me. I wanted to head to warmer climates and to places that I felt would be a better environment for my son, Ryan, who was born that same year. So, I sent out audition tapes and landed a job as sports anchor for KHOU-TV, Channel 11, in Houston.

I loved the idea of going to Texas and the early 1980s were great years to be in Houston. John Travolta released *Urban Cowboy* and the cowboy craze swept across America—it was popular for Texas to be "cowboy" country. We had the Houston Oilers and Bum Phillips. We had the world's biggest rodeo in Houston and people everywhere were wearing boots, jeans, and cowboy hats. I loved it!

In Houston, I did the sports at five o'clock and ten o'clock. One night, and I don't remember why, I went to a Wednesday night church service between sportscasts. Up until that night, I attended the Catholic church with my wife. But that night, I found myself at First Baptist of Houston with Dr. John Bisagno preaching. I had never heard a Baptist preacher before that night. I don't mind telling you, I felt as if he was talking directly to me. I kept glancing around, wondering how he knew my problems and whether anybody else realized he was only talking to me!

Let me make it very clear that I'm not trying to be an advocate for the Baptist church. It fits me, but it may not fit you. I don't care what church you attend, although I do recommend that you find a church that preaches Jesus and believes the Bible and that you attend regularly. There are many advantages to getting involved in a church. My goal in this book is to help you get into a personal relationship with God and develop a love for reading the Word of God. As you read the Word of God, I trust you will become convinced that you need to avail yourself of church-related opportunities for worship, Bible study, and good Bible teaching. A few weeks after I first attended First Baptist Church, I was baptized and joined the church.

About a year later I went to Dr. Bisagno and told him I was interested in possibly becoming a full-time pastor. He encouraged me, but told me that I could have more of an impact as a Christian leader in broadcasting. He told me that the world needed strong Christian leaders in all walks of life and in every business from politics to truck driving. I decided not to pursue a career as a pastor. Instead, I took his advice to heart and decided to try to be the best Christian I could be every day, and not just on Sunday. Even so, it would be over fourteen more years before I *fully* committed my life to the Lord and began serious Bible study.

I knew that if I was really going to get to know God...I needed to know the Bible. But I failed to get involved in a Bible study or Sunday school. I failed to start reading the Bible for myself. Many churchgoers and new Christians behave as I did. Today, I fully understand and appreciate what I did not understand then. Don't make my mistake. Get with the Word now, not later.

THE BIBLE IS THE PRIMARY WAY GOD "SPEAKS" TO US

The Bible is the way God reveals Himself to us. He may use other means from time to time, but the one sure-fire way that is consistently available to every man, woman, boy, and girl is the Bible. The Bible tells us…

- **Who God Is**. The Bible reveals His nature, His identity, and His motivations and purposes. The Bible uses a number of names for God. Each one reveals a little different facet of God's nature.

- **Who We Are**. The Bible holds up a mirror to us and says, "This is who you are as a human being." The Bible says that we all are like "sheep" who have gone astray from God, our Great Shepherd. The Bible tells us that we are in need of a Savior. The Bible tells us that we discover more about who we are and what God has called us to become through our DOING what the Bible tells us to do. The Bible says, "Be doers of the word, and not hearers only, deceiving yourselves. For if anyone is a hearer of the word and not a doer, he is like a man observing his natural face in a mirror; for he observes himself, goes away, and immediately forgets what kind of man he was. But he who looks into the perfect law of liberty and continues in it, and is not a forgetful hearer but a doer of the work, this one will be blessed in what he does." (James 1:22–24)

- **How to Have a Relationship with God**. The Bible tells us how to have a relationship with God, our Creator, Savior, and Lord.

- **How to Have a Good Relationship with Other People**. The Bible gives a ton of advice about how to have good relationships with other people—a spouse, children, parents, siblings, co-workers, pastors, fellow church workers, civil authorities, neighbors, and even strangers.

Every person on the earth today needs to know who God is, more about who he or she is as a person, how to have a relationship with God, and how to have good relationships with other people. If for no other reason, the Bible is HIGHLY APPLICABLE to your life today in these four areas!

- Do you know God today?

- Do you truly know yourself?

- Do you know how to get into right relationship with God?

- Do you know how BEST to treat other people around you?

The Bible has answers.

They are applicable to you.

And by the way, if you want to read the Bible version of the headlines offered at the beginning of this chapter, go to...

- 2 Samuel 11

- Matthew 26:14–16

- Genesis 37–38

- 2 Chronicles 20

- 2 Samuel 21:1–14

- Acts 27

And if you want to read more about the storylines mentioned at the beginning of this chapter, check out

- 1 Kings 21

- Exodus 1–2

- 2 Samuel 13

- Numbers 13

- Numbers 12

All of these passages are *highly* relevant to today. They talk about things that are happening all around us, sometimes at the highest levels and sometimes in the privacy of the homes in your neighborhood! Perhaps even in your own home.

5

EXCUSE #3

"BUT DAN... HOW DO I KNOW THE BIBLE IS TRUE?"

Years ago, I made a quantum leap in my thinking about God and the Bible. I went from "believing in God" to "believing God." I want you to pause and think about that statement. It is a profound life-changing proposition.

I had to decide for myself if the Bible is true. I wasn't about to change my life for something I didn't believe was true!

I am not an attorney. However, I occasionally like to role-play the part of an attorney when I make various arguments. If the evidence fits, I must commit. Here is what I would say as a "closing argument" on the issue of whether the Bible is the true Word of God. You are the jury and you must decide on my case.

Ladies and Gentlemen of the Jury:

At first, I began to study the Bible as just a book. The Bible is actually sixty-six books, thirty-nine in what is called the Old

Testament and twenty-seven in the New Testament. (In some circles the Old Testament is called the Hebrew Scriptures—for the Jews, the Old Testament *is* the Bible. The New Testament is called the Christian Scriptures.)

Most of the Old Testament was written originally in the Hebrew language. Most of the New Testament was written originally in Greek. The word *Biblia* means "books" in Greek.

The Bible was written over a period of approximately 1,500 years by thirty-five to forty authors.

MANY AUTHORS BUT ONE CONSISTENT MESSAGE

What is amazing is that there is *one and only one* consistent message throughout the entire Bible: God had a plan to redeem sinful mankind, and that plan ultimately was fulfilled by His Son, Jesus Christ.

The New Testament states: "When the fullness of the time had come, God sent forth His Son, born of a woman, born under the law, to redeem those who were under the law, that we might receive the adoption as sons. And because you are sons, God has sent forth the Spirit of His Son into your hearts, crying out, 'Abba, Father!'" (Gal. 4:4–6)

The New Testament also says, "God, who is rich in mercy, because of His great love with which He loved us, even when we were dead in trespasses, made us alive together with Christ (by grace you have been saved)." (Eph. 2:4–5)

I started to think as I read the Bible about how so many different people, over such a long period of time, could write a book that had one consistent message. All of this writing had occurred before computers, copy machines, or even books. If today, with all of our technology, we set out to write a book over the next 1,500 years, choosing 40 writers, we could hardly expect that it would be humanly possible to end up with one coherent singular message. The ego of the writers alone would foul up the process!

The earliest writings of the Old Testament were on scrolls. We do not have any of these earliest documents today. However, we do have some Old Testament fragments that are more than two thousand years old.

In a remarkable find in caves near the Dead Sea, a group of scrolls subsequently called the Dead Sea Scrolls were found in 1947. These were second-century copies of the Old Testament. Up until then, the oldest Hebrew Old Testament manuscripts that were known to exist were from the ninth and tenth centuries. When the manuscripts were compared, they matched perfectly, illustrating how carefully the first scribes (those whose job it was to handwrite copies of the manuscripts) had done their job over hundreds of years. We also know that according to the New Testament, Jesus recognized the Old Testament as the Word of God.

In 1979, the oldest pieces of the Bible were found in Jerusalem. They go back to about the time that Jerusalem was destroyed by the Babylonians (about 600 BC). These fragments bear the citation, "Numbers 6:22–27."

Lastly, we have the Septuagint. This was the Greek translation of the Old Testament made in about 250 BC.

Between 15,000 and 24,000 pieces of New Testament documents have been dated back to the time just after the death of Jesus Christ. (The counting differs according to whether fragments, entire manuscripts, or copied portions are being counted.) Early translations into other languages are also available.

STILL MORE EVIDENCE

The New Testament developed from eyewitness accounts of the life and death of Jesus Christ.

In approximately 400 AD, Jerome translated the Bible into Latin. This Bible was called the Vulgate and it became the standard Bible of the Roman Catholic Church for the next several hundred years.

As I analyzed this Book of all books, the Holy Bible, it seemed implausible and impossible that multiple authors, over hundreds of years, and devoid of modern technology, could collaborate on a book that was roughly 2,000 pages long with *one* consistent message. Not only is the message consistent, but the identities of various people, places, and events are consistent against nonbiblical historical records!

We have countless historical documents substantiating the text as authentic. In fact, there are more documents to validate the Bible than there are documents that exist on any one person, place, or event in all history. People have accepted "facts" about a vast number of people and events in history on far less documentation!

Furthermore, prophecies were consistently fulfilled from one time period to the next. In all, the internal consistency of the Bible is amazing. I must conclude that such consistency was not an achievement accomplished by man alone.

In looking at the writings themselves, *if the Bible was not the inspired Word of God,* then the mortal men who wrote it must have been the smartest, wisest men who ever lived.

The fact is, despite the limited education of ancient times, no one since the writing of the Bible has been able to improve on their work. No one person or group of people has written anything close to the great teachings of the Bible in the last two thousand years. No document so clearly spells out right from wrong, within a context of love, forgiveness, and divine purpose. The Bible has been the foundation for all legal systems that advocate genuine personal freedom for the last three thousand years.

REAL PEOPLE AND REAL PLACES

What about the places in the Bible? Archaeologists have not been able to find archaeological ruins of *every* place mentioned in the Bible...at least, not thus far. However, most places either still exist or have been recorded in other historical documents as existing at one time. The key city in the Bible is Jerusalem. The Bible predicted the Jews would return to their land. Who in the 1940s, as the Jews were being killed by the millions in the Holocaust, could have dreamed that Israel would exist today as the modern, thriving nation that it is? The Bible further predicts that Jerusalem and the land surrounding it will one day be at the center of Christ's return to the earth.

The same holy sites described in the Bible thousands of years ago still exist today, either as thriving cities or as ruins.

Members of the jury, I trust you will agree with me on the validity of the Bible based on this first set of conclusions. Let me move on to the key question of whether Jesus Christ is the true Son of God.

There is ample Scripture, some of which we have already addressed, that says that Jesus is the one and only Son of God sent to earth, so that whoever believes in Him shall be saved and have everlasting life. The question for many people is this: "Can I believe the story of Jesus told in the four Gospels: Matthew, Mark, Luke, and John?"

EYEWITNESSES TO THE TRUTH

Let's analyze this one aspect of the Bible. In all, some twelve disciples and other eyewitnesses told the story of Jesus firsthand to the four men whose names are associated with the Gospels. Matthew and John were direct eyewitnesses to His life. They were among Jesus' chosen twelve disciples, also called apostles. The Gospel of Mark is believed to have been written by John Mark, who was a witness to some of the life and death and resurrection of Jesus—John Mark was a traveling companion of the apostle Peter. The Gospel of Luke (as well as the book titled Acts of the Apostles) is believed to have been written by a man named Luke who was a member of the first-century Christian church and a close traveling companion of the apostle Paul. Many believe that during the two years that Paul was imprisoned in Caesarea, Luke had the opportunity to interview a number of the first disciples and other eyewitness followers of Jesus, including Mary, the mother of Jesus.

Apart from the Gospels, many of the letters and other books that make up the New Testament were written by the apostle Paul, a prolific writer and one of the most serious evangelists and teachers in the decades that immediately followed the death of Jesus. Several letters and the Book of Revelation were written by the apostle John (who also wrote the Gospel of John).

DO YOU STILL DOUBT?

One of Jesus' closest followers had to be "convinced" that Jesus had risen from the dead. The word of his fellow apostles wasn't sufficient—Thomas wanted to see the nail prints in Jesus' hands and feet. Hence, he has been called "doubting Thomas" through the centuries. In fact, he should perhaps more accurately be called "evidence-demanding Thomas."

There is nothing wrong with honest doubt, which is a demanding of evidence before believing. Jesus answered Thomas' request for evidence by appearing to him, along with other apostles, and saying to Thomas, "Reach your finger here, and look at My hands; and reach your hand here, and put it into My side. Do not be unbelieving, but believing." And Thomas answered and said to Him, 'My Lord and my God!'" (See John 20:27–28.)

Honest doubt asks questions and seeks evidence. Doubt only becomes negative when a person *refuses* to believe without fully seeking answers.

The Bible tells about a number of doubters. Moses doubted that God had chosen the right person to lead the Children of Israel out of Egypt. Abraham doubted he would be a father in his old age— and his wife Sarah certainly doubted that she would be a mother. The Israelites frequently expressed doubt that God was leading them through the wilderness and would provide fully for their material and physical needs.

Who is ultimately behind lingering doubt? Satan. The first person in whom he sought to establish doubt was Eve in the Garden of Eden. Satan's ploy then, as now, is to plant questions in the mind about God.

Our role is to seek answers to those questions without buying the questions wholesale and allowing the questions to mislead us into *not* believing.

The Bible says, "If any of you lacks wisdom, let him ask of God, who gives to all liberally and without reproach, and it will be given to him. But let him ask in faith, with no doubting, for he who doubts is like a wave of the sea driven and tossed by the wind. For let not that man suppose that he will receive anything from the Lord; he is a double-minded man, unstable in all his ways." (James 1:5–8)

Eleven of the twelve apostles, including Thomas, and other eyewitnesses who told the story of Christ all died horrific deaths at the hands of unbelievers. That begs the question: If these men did not truly believe what they saw, would they have been willing to die painful, hideous deaths for a made-up story? I don't know anyone who is willing to die for something he knows isn't true. I certainly have never heard about an entire group of people dying for a story they knew to be false, especially a group scattered in various locations and separated for a number of years. People just don't die for practical jokes.

The apostles were extremely passionate in their retelling the story of Jesus. Their account of His life, death, and resurrection led to the establishment of the first church—the earliest group of Christian believers. The movement they began hasn't stopped growing in the last two thousand years. Many of the people who heard the first apostles and believed their message also died horrendous deaths rather than deny the truth of Jesus as the Son of God.

The leaders of Rome attempted a wholesale slaughter of Christians at the hands of gladiators, lions, and even worse death scenarios. As much as they tried to eradicate Christianity, they succeeded only in changing the entire Empire into a Christian nation! Martyrs through the ages have died rather than deny the lordship of Jesus and His statement, "I am the way, the truth, and the life. No one comes to the Father except through Me." (John 14:6)

Throughout the Middle East and Europe, a traveler can visit amazing churches that were built hundreds, even almost two thousand years ago. The people who built these churches often gave up all their possessions and even their lives to establish places of worship to Jesus, the Son of God.

Ladies and Gentlemen of the Jury: Based upon the evidence presented to you, I ask you to find that the Bible is true…that Jesus IS who He said He was and is … and that the Bible must be *believed*. Any other conclusion simply ignores the amount of credible evidence.

WHEN DID THINGS START TO GO WRONG?

People who choose NOT to believe that the Bible is true nearly always have troubled lives. I'm not judging them. I'm just telling it as I see it. I have encountered dozens of people who adamantly state that they don't believe the Bible can be trusted to be the truth…and in EVERY CASE, the person admitted that at one point in their lives they thought the Bible was true (or that it might be true) but then they decided it wasn't true. Some have said,"The Bible just didn't WORK for me, Dan."And in EVERY CASE, from the time the person decided the Bible wasn't true— their lives took a downward spiral. Relationships crumbled in some cases. Businesses fell apart in others. Health deteriorated for some. Troubles and addictions and inner turmoil escalated!

I can't help but conclude from their lives that they should have continued to believe!

WHEN TERRY BRADSHAW HAD HAIR

Occasionally when I look back over my life, I feel as if I'm something of a real-life Forrest Gump. I have been part of or been a

THE SECOND MOST IMPORTANT BOOK YOU'LL EVER READ

witness to many life experiences that I never could have dreamed I would witness. I've met, and in some cases become friends with people I never imagined I'd meet or know, including presidents, politicians, astronauts, athletes, celebrities, millionaires, billionaires, and some of the most outstanding Christian leaders of our time. In most cases, I was merely a spectator sharing a brief moment with them. In some cases, I had face-to-face and conversational encounters. Let me tell you about one such encounter.

In 1980, I went to the Los Angeles area to cover Super Bowl XIV between the Los Angeles Rams and the Pittsburgh Steelers. On the plane, I read an article in a Christian publication about the Steelers' star quarterback, Terry Bradshaw. The article indicated that Terry had grown up as a Christian, but had lost sight of the Lord once he made it into the NFL. His story was of particular interest to me since I was having problems walking out in a practical way what I believed to be true and right in my heart.

In those days, the way pregame coverage worked was this. Various players would come into a large room. Each player would take a seat at a different table—usually they were round tables that seated ten people. Each table would have a sign on it with the name of the player who would be seated there. Sportscasters and commentators would then try to get as close as possible to the table of the players they most wanted to interview—the ideal place, of course, was to get a seat at the table assigned to that player.

Since there were hundreds of media representatives at the Super Bowl, I knew it would be hard to get a place at Terry Bradshaw's table. So, I went to the press event *three hours early* to ensure that I got a seat at his table. I put up the chair next to me against the table as if to "save" that seat. I knew other reporters would sit at the empty seats. And in the end, by the time Terry arrived, there was no place for him to sit except at the seat I had "saved" next to me!

I listened for a while to the questions about the upcoming game. Then I asked, "Terry, tell me about Christ in your life." Suddenly the table became very quiet. I heard a couple of reporters groan, as if to say "who is this guy and what kind of question is that?" Terry looked at me and didn't say a word. I didn't know what might happen next.

Then he smiled and said, "I'm glad you asked that question." He went on to say how he had neglected his walk with the Lord when he made it big in the NFL. He talked about how he came to a time when he just couldn't seem to find his receivers, John Stallworth and Lynn Swann, in the pass pattern. He talked about how he had been booed because of his bad play. He told how all of this caused him to reexamine his life and ask what had changed. It was then he realized he had left God out of his life. He made a decision to once again put God first, as he had been taught as a young man when he was at home. And suddenly, he said, his game came back. He started hitting receivers with pinpoint accuracy. The team started winning games and both the fans and sports reporters began to cheer him again.

Very quickly, the reporters at the table began to write feverishly. I personally have never forgotten that day or Terry Bradshaw's words. Later in my own life, when I found myself asking myself what was different in my life and why I seemed to be unhappy and struggling, I remembered Terry's words. And like Terry, when I asked God to come back into my life, I started to hit the long passes of *my* life into the end zone.

By the way, Bradshaw's Steelers won that season's Super Bowl 31–19 and he was named the Most Valuable Player of the game.

BELIEVING ISN'T ALWAYS EASY

Some things in the Bible simply can't be understood apart from BELIEF. That's true for every aspect of our relationship with God. I have found time and time again that when I choose to "believe

God"—believing the Bible is true and that God is speaking to me through the Bible—I have found that not only do I understand more of what the Bible says, but I also find more ways to apply the Bible to my life. The end result is that I see more EVIDENCE in my own personal experience that the Bible is true. What we experience for ourselves, we *know* to be true. Nobody can convince us otherwise.

The Bible never makes the claim that believing is the "easy route" or that everybody will believe. Jesus taught, "Enter by the narrow gate; for wide is the gate and broad is the way that leads to destruction, and there are many who go in by it. Because narrow is the gate and difficult is the way which leads to life, and there are few who find it." (Matt. 7:13–14)

Jesus also said, "I am the door of the sheep." (John 10:7) He continued, "I am the door. If anyone enters by Me, he will be saved, and will go in and out and find pasture." (John 10:9)

No…not everybody will believe. Not everybody will seek answers to their questions born of doubt. Not everybody will ask God for truth, and seek it until they find it.

The good news, however, is that ALL who seek to believe WILL be given the answers they need. Jesus also said, "Ask, and it will be given to you; seek, and you will find; knock, and it will be opened to you. For everyone who asks receives, and he who seeks finds, and to him who knocks it will be opened." (Matt. 7:7–8)

Jesus was not talking about material goods, a job, a mate, or other worldly things. He was talking about the truth of Himself. People who give up after a brief attempt or two at reaching out to God are not those who are truly asking, seeking, or knocking. The tense of those words in the Greek is one that implies continual action: "Ask and keep on asking"…"seek and keep on seeking"…"knock and keep on knocking." Those who persist in searching for the truth about God— Father, Son, and Holy Spirit—*will find* the truth about God. They will also discover for themselves the truth of God's Word, the Bible.

6

EXCUSE #4

"BUT DAN...I ALREADY KNOW RIGHT FROM WRONG"

The fourth big excuse that I hear from people for not reading the Bible is this:"I already know right from wrong."These people see the Bible as primarily a "rule book." And the fact is, they don't like the rules. They might want to play by some of them, but not all of them. And along the way, they don't want any guilt trips.

I don't know anybody who enjoys living with guilt or shame. And let's face it, everybody who is running from God has guilt or shame lurking in them at some level and in some area of their life.

I also don't know many people who enjoy face-to-face encounters with truth. I don't know anybody who *wants* to put an end to their living the way *they* want to live.

Except for the truly evil people in the world, most people still have a semblance of a conscience and know right from wrong. They feel little pangs of remorse, shame, fear, embarrassment, or guilt when they do wrong. But...they are hoping that those feelings will go away and that God will overlook their failures and faults. They are scared that God might require something of them, and in particular, require a change that goes against their own way of believing and behaving. Pride is tough to lay down.

Human beings have an amazing capacity to "plead ignorance" and "hope for the best" when it concerns their own misdeeds. They have a great desire to believe that somehow, in some way, they will do more good than harm in life and the scale of justice will fall in their favor.

Such people believe that by being a "good person," they will get to heaven after they die. In short, they are placing *their* standard of fairness on God and are not accepting His Word on the subject.

Frankly, I think that's a huge risk to take.

The fact is, good deeds rarely accomplish what we hope they will. Most of them are overlooked, under-rewarded, and can even be twisted and warped so that they aren't even "good" in the eyes of some people.

So... if most of us know right from wrong, why read the Bible?

Well, in the first place, what many people believe is righteous living simply isn't. The Bible tells us WHY we need to remind ourselves of right from wrong. And it also gives us understanding about WHY God calls some things wrong. In both cases, this information is very much for our benefit!

The Bible says:

> If you receive my words,
> And treasure my commands within you,
> So that you incline your ear to wisdom,
> And apply your heart to understanding;
> Yes, if you cry out for discernment,
> And lift up your voice for understanding,

If you seek her as silver,
And search for her as for hidden treasures;
Then you will understand the fear of the Lord,
And find the knowledge of God....
Then you will understand righteousness and justice,
Equity and every good path.
When wisdom enters your heart,
And knowledge is pleasant to your soul,
Discretion will preserve you;
Understanding will keep you.
(Prov. 2:1–5, 9–11)

PRESIDENT BUSH AND ME

Dr. Ed Young, my pastor, is a man upon whom President George W. Bush (that's #43) has called upon occasionally for spiritual guidance. Before becoming president, then Texas Governor Bush gave his personal testimony at Second Baptist Church in Houston one week. He told how his life was changed by accepting Jesus Christ as his Savior.

Like many others and me, President Bush came to the Lord later in life. By his own published accounts, he went to Billy Graham and asked what he could do to find peace and happiness. Dr. Graham led George to Christ.

I do not claim to be a personal friend of the president. However, because our radio station covered almost a third of southeast Texas voters, the former Governor Bush was familiar with our stations and with me. I interviewed him on several occasions.

In May 1999, I was invited to attend a small luncheon with the governor in Dallas. I had a chance to spend a few informal and very personal minutes one-on-one with him. We talked about our mutual walk with the Lord and how we both came to a committed faith later in our lives. I haven't talked to the president since, but I remember leaving that luncheon feeling ecstatic that the governor of my state truly had committed his life to Jesus Christ.

I take comfort today in our war against terrorism that the man who is leading our nation and the free world in this fight is a man who sincerely prays every day, asking God for guidance.

Many of our presidents, both Democrat and Republican, have very publicly gone to church or have invited clergy into the White House. From what these former presidents have said and done, however, I cannot help but question whether they truly *believed* what they claimed to believe.

Former presidents, of course, are not the only ones who might be questioned on this point. There are countless people across our nation who carry their Bibles openly, show up at church on Christmas and Easter, and tip the collection plate at the appropriate time. Their knowledge of God's Word, however, is paper thin. I know. I once was just that way.

You may be saying, "That sounds very judgmental, Dan."

Well, one of the main reasons for knowing what God's Word says is so that we *can* judge. But read me very closely on this. Judgment according to God's Word may not at all be what *you* think is judgment!

WHO'S TO JUDGE?

Judgment is one of the most misunderstood principles of the Bible. Usually, the topic of judgment is taken out of context or is totally missed. I find that the media especially seems to be gifted in mangling the message of forgiveness that is associated with the topic of judgment.

I don't judge a person's soul, heart, or salvation. None of us knows with certainty who might be in heaven with us. Jesus said about this, "Again, the kingdom of heaven is like a dragnet that was cast into the sea and gathered some of every kind, which, when it was full, they drew to shore; and they sat down and gathered the good into vessels, but threw the bad away. So it will be at the end of the age. The angels will come forth, separate the wicked from among the just, and cast them into the furnace of fire. There will be wailing and gnashing of teeth." (Matt. 13:47–50) Jesus clearly taught that it is not up to us to judge who will or will not be in heaven.

As much as we cannot and must not judge the motives, thoughts, intents, or spiritual decisions of another person...we are to judge behavior or actions, including words. We are to judge behavior according to God's standards of right and wrong, and to speak out against wrong at appropriate times, in an appropriate manner, in appropriate places, and most importantly, with an attitude of love.

We are also to judge *deeds* against the criterion of God's Word taken as a *whole*. We are not to take deeds out of context or fail to seek an understanding of the *whole* of what Jesus taught. We cannot be halfhearted in following God's Word, or have a half-baked understanding of what is truth.

Jesus said, "I know your *works*, that you are neither cold nor hot. I could wish you were cold or hot. So then, because you are lukewarm, and neither cold nor hot, I will spew you out of My mouth." (Rev. 3:15–16)

The church and its members must speak out against evil whenever it is appropriate to do so.

FIRST JUDGE
YOUR OWN SELF

The Bible is very clear that we should not judge the words or actions of others unless we also FIRST judge our own words and actions. Jesus said, "Why do you look at the speck in your brother's eye, but do not consider the plank in your own eye?" (Matt. 7:3) Jesus also said, "Judge not, that you be not judged. For with what judgment you judge, you will be judged; and with the same measure you use, it will be measured back to you." (Matt. 7:1–2)

What applies at the individual level also applies at the level of the church as a whole in addressing the behavior of those who are NOT in the church. The apostle Paul, one of the most prolific writers of the New Testament, wrote about problems in the church in Corinth: "For what have I to do with judging those also who are outside? Do you not judge those who are inside? But those who are outside God judges. Therefore, 'put away from yourselves that wicked person.'" (1 Cor. 5:12–13)

We are not to associate with evil. The expulsion of "the wicked person" refers to those who willfully and repeatedly engage in evil deeds even though they have been admonished by fellow believers to change their behavior. (See 1 Cor. 5:1–11.)

In judging wicked behavior, we are never to talk behind a person's back (gossip) or immediately jump in and harshly tell people to change their behavior in the presence of others. We first are to go to them privately, and then if they refuse to hear us, take just one other person with us.

We are, however, to speak up about problems we see within the Christian community. That involves a whole range of moral issues (such as child abuse by religious leaders and unbiblical fund-raising tactics or misappropriation of funds by church officials). We are to be on our guard against any person who pretends to stand for God but is actually a deceiver.

Where is our judgment to lead?

The Bible says that the end destination for good judgment is twofold:

- Greater wholeness—a greater sense of completion and harmony in our personal lives: body, mind, spirit, and relationships. Wholeness is not just for individuals. It is also for groups of people who desire to live in obedience to God. In other words, it is for the Body of Christ or the church.

- A greater awareness of the relationship God desires to have for us.

Let's explore this a little more.

A MATTER OF PERSONAL PERFECTION OR WHOLENESS

I am far from perfect.

Guess what? So is every other person—Christian or not.

The only perfect person who ever walked this earth was Jesus.

What I and all other genuine Christians know with great clarity is that we *aren't* perfect. We know we are sinners in need of forgiveness. We know we are in the process of being transformed into a growing likeness of Christ's character.

If I make a mistake...I want to try to correct it.

If I lose my temper...I want to be quick to apologize.

If I become angry...I want to experience God's peace.

If I become envious...I want to trust God to give me what He wants me to have.

If I find myself becoming too involved in worldly matters...I ask God to show me *His* plan, *His* method, *His* way.

If I offend or take advantage of another person...I want to ask for their forgiveness and seek a means of restitution. I want always to be quick to ask for forgiveness and to ask the Holy Spirit to impart to me the strength to be an overcomer of any evil attack against my life.

How can any of us move from our imperfections to a more complete or "whole" state of being? The Bible says we do this by confronting our own sin and errors...by changing our direction, choosing to move away from sin and toward God...and by lining up our lives according to God's commandments and principles. In other words, by "judging" our own behavior.

A MATTER
OF RELATIONSHIP

A second reason to judge our own behavior is so we can grow in our understanding of God and develop an ongoing relationship with Him.

Some of the obvious conclusions that we must come to when we judge our own behavior are these:

- God is infinite and we are not.

- God is all-powerful and we are not.

- God is all wise and we are not.

- God is eternal and we are very much time-bound.

- God is Spirit and we are flesh.

None of us is God and never will be. He is the Creator and we are the created beings.

And there's one more truth that comes shining through when we judge ourselves against the standard of God's Word: God is all loving, with a steadfast and unconditional love. We are not.

Judgment of our own lives brings us face to face with the fact of God's love, the very heart of His nature.

GOD'S INFINITE LOVE FOR US

The one consistent message of the Bible from cover to cover is this: God loves us and desires to forgive us so we can spend all of eternity with Him. In a nutshell, that's God's plan for every person who has been born. It is God's nature to love us. It is His desire to forgive us. It is His goal to bring us to the point of our saying "yes" to His free offer of salvation. (See the segment on definitions in Chapter 17, found in Section 3.)

The Bible says that God loved you and me so much that He was willing to sacrifice His only Son for us. I don't know what kind of love you have experienced in your life, but I've never known anyone who would be willing to sacrifice his or her child—or put that child through a terrible death—in order to help someone else. In my opinion, the fact that God loved us so much that He sent Jesus to die on a cross in our place is the most awesome fact of history. God's love is a love that is almost unfathomable, unthinkable, unknowable. It is a love greater than any human love.

The message of the Bible begins with God's love and is ultimately about God's love. It is about God's desire that we love others and that we love ourselves (for the way God made us and the purpose He has planned for us). It is also about how we are to love our enemies. From cover to cover, the Bible is a love story.

I challenge you to look up these passages in the Bible and read God's Word for yourself:

- Romans 5:5
- Romans 8:38–39
- 2 Corinthians 13
- 1 John 3:11–17
- 1 John 4:7–21

The Bible has many other verses about love. I encourage you to seek them out!

Actually, it would take countless libraries if one were to tell ALL the stories of God's love manifested through the ages. There's a story of God's love for every person ever born ... every relationship ever forged ... every act of goodness ever done!

Remember this: God loves you more than you can possibly imagine. He sacrificed His only begotten Son because He loved *you* so much He wants you to be forgiven of your sins and live with Him forever. Jesus said of Himself, "Greater love has no one than this, than to lay down one's life for his friends." (John 15:13)

The Bible also says, "Behold, what manner of love the Father has bestowed on us, that we should be called children of God!" (1 John 3:1)

RELATIONSHIP MORE THAN RITUAL

Jesus was not particularly concerned about religion or ritual. He was mostly concerned about *relationship*. The religious leaders of His day, called the Pharisees and Sadducees, were very strict in their approach to religion. The word "Pharisee" means "separated one," and that's the way the Pharisees saw themselves—as being separated and "above" other people who did not keep religious laws to the same degree of perfection that they sought to keep them. Their laws did not begin and end with the Law of Moses in the Bible, but included hundreds of non-Bible laws that had been added by religious people through the centuries after the Law of Moses was given to the Israelites.

The Pharisees could not understand how a rabbi (teacher) named Jesus would bother going to where low-life sinners hung out. They questioned everything Jesus did because He seemed to include with generosity many whom they did not believe were worthy of God's attention, much less God's love.

The Pharisees questioned strongly Jesus' actions on the Sabbath day. They believed His miracle healings were tantamount to *work*, which was unlawful in keeping the Sabbath holy. On one occasion, a group of Pharisees point-blank asked Jesus, "Why are you doing what is unlawful on the Sabbath?"

Jesus reminded them that King David and his men had once eaten the bread that had been consecrated for use in the holy tabernacle because they were hungry. Jesus said, "The Son of Man is also Lord of the Sabbath." (You can read about this in Luke 6:2–5.)

This didn't mean that Jesus was opposed to the commandments of God. Not at all! Rather, He saw that all of the commandments of God were given by God out of a motivation of love, and that all of the commandments of God were for the *good* of mankind. The commandments of God were a hallmark of the loving relationship that God sought to have with man. We are to obey God's commandments because they put us into a position to receive God's best and highest blessings. God gave His commands and God blesses us out of a heart overflowing with infinite love, tenderness, mercy, and a desire to see us, His beloved children, become and do all that we have been created to be and do!

Jesus said:

> Do not think that I came to destroy the Law or the Prophets. I did not come to destroy but to fulfill. For assuredly, I say to you, till heaven and earth pass away, one jot or one tittle will by no means pass from the law till all is fulfilled. Whoever therefore breaks one of the least of these commandments, and teaches men so, shall be called least in the kingdom of heaven; but whoever does and teaches them, he shall be called great in the kingdom of heaven. For I say to you, that unless your righteousness exceeds the righteousness of the scribes and Pharisees, you will by no means enter the kingdom of heaven. (Matt. 5:17–20)

Jesus didn't dismiss the value of keeping God's Law or the teachings of the Prophets. He personally lived by those laws and teachings and taught others to live by them. What Jesus meant by a righteousness that exceeded or surpassed that of the Pharisees was that people were to keep the commandments out of LOVE for God, not fear or rigid religiosity.

Three types of law existed in Jesus' day: ceremonial law, civil law, and moral law. The Ten Commandments are an example of Old Testament moral law. The Pharisees' problem was that they looked and acted out the part of living the moral law, but didn't live out or portray the *spirit* in which that law was given. The law was given by

God with love. The Pharisees didn't extend the law to others with love, but rather, disdain.

Before any person can feel truly good about his outward actions, he must feel good about his inward relationships with God and others. And before he can feel good about his inward relationships, he must *know* that he is loved by God, forgiven by God, and fully accepted and counted as worthy by God. Once a person knows that he is loved, forgiven, and valued by God, it is EASY to live by God's commandments. All of the "have to" attitudes associated with the commandments are replaced by "want to" attitudes!

Jesus taught this: "If anyone loves Me, he will keep My word; and My Father will love him, and We will come to him and make Our home with him. He who does not love Me does not keep My words." (John 14:23–24)

The Bible teaches that we are to love God. But that isn't all!

Jesus once was asked to state the most important commandment. He said:

> The first of all the commandments is: "Hear, O Israel, the LORD our God, the LORD is one. And you shall love the LORD your God with all your heart, with all your soul, with all your mind, and with all your strength." This is the first commandment. And the second, like it, is this: "You shall love your neighbor as yourself." There is no other commandment greater than these. (Mark 12:29–31)

The concept of love is one that many people seem to have difficulty with when it comes to God. They see God as a judge, harsh and punitive. It's amazing to me, however, that these same people see JESUS as being loving, forgiving, and kind, especially as He healed people, delivered them from demons, and sought to teach them the way to have their lives significantly improved. Let us never forget that Jesus said of Himself, "He who has seen Me has seen the Father; so how can you say, 'Show us the Father?' Do you not believe that I am in the Father, and the Father in Me? The words that I speak to you I do not speak on My own authority; but the Father who dwells in Me does the works. Believe Me that I am in the Father and the Father in Me, or else believe Me for the sake of the works themselves." (John 14:9–11)

Even more problematic for many people is the Bible's teaching that we are to love our enemies. How can a person love those who hurt him, or bring harm to the ones he cares most deeply about? How can we love those who persecute us?

Jesus was very clear in addressing questions such as these. He said:

> You have heard that it was said, "You shall love your neighbor and hate your enemy." But I say to you, love your enemies, bless those who curse you, do good to those who hate you, and pray for those who spitefully use you and persecute you, that you may be sons of your Father in heaven; for He makes His sun rise on the evil and on the good, and sends rain on the just and on the unjust. For if you love those who love you, what reward have you? Do not even the tax collectors do the same? And if you greet your brethren only, what do you do more than others? Do not even the tax collectors do so? Therefore you shall be perfect, just as your Father in heaven is perfect. (Matt. 5:43–48)

Let me point out just a couple of things from this passage. In saying God causes the "sun to rise" on the evil and the good means that God gives TIME to both evil and good people. Sometimes bad people live long lives, and sometimes good people live short lives. God determines the time each of us has on this earth. When we read that

God sends "rain" to the righteous and unrighteous, we must remember that rain was and is one of the greatest blessings in the area of Israel. Desert people needed rain to have drinking water, to plant and irrigate their crops, and to water their livestock. Rain was vital for life! Jesus was pointing out that sometimes the unrighteous seem to be blessed with great blessings, and sometimes the most godly people have little material wealth. God determines the "blessings" each of us receives.

Our part is not to seek to extend our lives or further our own material wealth as much as it is to show LOVE to others. In this we differ greatly from the unrighteous (ungodly) people. We are to love not only those who love us and do good to us, but to love those who persecute or hurt us.

Jesus said that we are to be "perfect" as God is perfect. You may be saying, "That's not possible!" You're right. But the problem here is that we have a different meaning for the word "perfect" than the people in Jesus' day. To be "perfect" means to be whole and to be forgiven and cleansed of sin. Jesus said that we MUST forgive if we are to be forgiven and cleansed of sin...and to be "whole" in the Father's eyes.

To love our enemies does NOT mean that we turn away and never insist that those who harm us be held responsible for their actions. God is *just*, even as He is loving. What it means is that we need to *forgive* those who hurt us—which means to let them go from the shackles of our heart and to let God mete out His justice when and how He wants to give justice, including through the method of a court of law. It means that we are to *love* our enemies in a very practical way.

The Bible says, "Bless those who persecute you; bless and do not curse." (Rom. 12:14) In other words, we are to speak well of, and do good to, those who seek our harm. The Bible also says:

Repay no one evil for evil. Have regard for good things in the sight of all men. If it is possible, as much as depends on you, live peaceably with all men. Beloved, do not avenge yourselves, but rather give place to wrath; for it is written, "Vengeance is Mine, I will repay," says the Lord. Therefore

"If your enemy is hungry, feed him;

If he is thirsty, give him a drink;

For in so doing you will heap coals of fire on his head."

Do not be overcome by evil, but overcome evil with good. (Rom. 12:17–21)

LOVE AT THE VERY HEART OF JUDGMENT

The bottom line is this: When we judge ourselves against the standards of God's Word, we each must face the truth that we are not particularly lovable or loving, that we are desperately in need of God's love, and we aren't very good at loving others apart from our FIRST experiencing God's love.

The bottom line of judgment—the beginning and the end of it—is God's love.

It is the bright searing light of God's unconditional love that awakens our eyes to our own sin. It is the great joy of His unconditional love that brands us as God's own. Love is God's motivation for reaching out to us. Love is to be our motivation for all that we do in life.

Yes, you may know right from wrong—in your head, as the truth of words on a page. But do you feel compelled to CHOOSE right over wrong? Do you truly know the difference between LOVE and a life without genuine love?

DAN'S TOP TEN BENEFITS OF BIBLE READING

God doesn't desire for you to read the Bible because it gives Him a good feeling. He desires for you to read it because knowing and applying the Bible's principles is *your* key to reaping major benefits in your life. As you benefit, your family members, friends, co-workers, and fellow church members will also benefit! God's desire is to *bless* His people.

The Bible is the key to finding out just how abundantly He desires to bless!

7

BENEFIT #1

GETTING RIGHT WITH GOD

For a number of years after I accepted Jesus as my Savior—from 1980 to 1994—I lived in what I now call my "pre-season" as a Christian. In professional football, the preseason games don't count. They are a time for practicing and determining who does and doesn't make the team. Looking back, my life didn't count for much in those years.

I stated earlier that I had tried to make a deal with God in the Scranton church that I would use my career as a platform for spreading God's Word if God would just give me a job in broadcasting. As in the story I shared about Terry Bradshaw, I forgot that "deal" for many years. I still believed in Jesus as the Son of God. But when it came to reading the Bible and doing what it said to do, I was highly negligent. I liked to think of the Ten Commandments as something of an a la carte menu. I liked living by Dan's rules instead of God's rules. I never did anything illegal or engaged in behaviors that could get me thrown in jail. But neither did I consistently behave as a Christian should.

The good news—actually the *great* news— is that even though I lost sight of God, He never lost sight of me. He didn't cut me from His team!

No matter what we do or don't do after we are saved, God never stops being the Head Coach. (See the definitions in Section 4 if you want to know what I mean about being "saved.") God is always waiting for us to get serious about giving our best to the plans and purposes He has for us. He is always waiting to encourage us to be all that He created us to be. He always wants to teach us and coach us to a huge "win" in the Christian life.

It doesn't make any difference who you are, what you have, what you know, or what you've done, God stands ready to love us, forgive us, and use us.

One of the most famous stories in the Bible is the story of a boy who made a serious mistake in his life. (You can read this story for yourself in Luke 15:11–32.) The story is about a man who had two sons. The older boy stayed with his father and helped him in his business and obeyed him. The younger son insisted that his father give him the portion of the estate he was to inherit one day, and then the younger son left home and went into an ungodly territory and lived a life according to his own rules and desires. In the end, he squandered all the money his father had given him. He was penniless and friendless. (That's usually the case, isn't it, when people only associate with you because you have money, fame, or things are going well for you?)

This boy ended up slopping pigs—he was so hungry even the husks he was feeding the hogs started to look good to him. He finally came to his senses and concluded, "Even the servants in my father's house live better than I'm living. I'll go home, ask my father to forgive me and make me a servant." He left the pigs and headed home.

As he approached his father's house, his father saw him coming down the road. And his father, filled with compassion, ran to him, threw his arms around him, and kissed him. All of these were very public signs of forgiveness, and the custom of that time was that if a father forgave his son, others in the community also needed to forgive.

The son started in on his speech, telling the father he was no longer worthy to be called a son. But the father interrupted him. He called his servants and ordered that a calf be butchered so a feast could be made in the boy's honor. He gave his son the best robe to wear at the feast, put a ring on his son's hand (signifying that the son would be allowed to conduct family business), and put shoes on his feet (which was a sign that the boy was *not* a servant, but a son with freedom to come and go from the family home as he desired). The father gave to his son *all* of the rights of being a full member of the family. He rejoiced as he did so, saying, "This son of mine was dead and is alive again; he was lost and is found."

Jesus told this story to a group of people who were very unforgiving. He told it not so much as a story about a boy who made a mistake, but rather, about a God who continues to love us and desires to forgive us no matter *what* we might do. No son in Jesus' time could sink lower than this boy sank. No son could "sin" more than this boy sinned. Yet the father freely and generously forgave him and restored him. This father never stopped loving his boy.

What a tremendous image this is of God's love for us!

What a tremendous encouragement this should be to us if we have a son or daughter, or any other person we dearly love, who is not serving the Lord and has gone astray!

I always feel sad when I hear people say that there are some things they believe can *not* be forgiven. That may be true, but not because the sins are unforgivable. The fact is, some people are not capable of forgiving some sins. But God is capable of forgiving *all* manner of sin, and all quantity of sin. There is no degree of sin, no type of sin, and no pattern of sin that He is unwilling to forgive. His only admonition as He forgives us is this: "Go and sin no more."

Jesus Didn't Come to Condemn Us

The Bible has another wonderful story of forgiveness. A woman was brought to Jesus after being caught in the act of adultery. (What happened to the man is not told!) The religious leaders brought her to Jesus to attempt to trick Jesus. They said to Him, "The law of Moses says that a woman caught in the act of adultery should be stoned to death. What do You say?"

Jesus knelt and began to write on the ground. They continued to question Him. Finally Jesus said to them, "If any one of you is without sin, let him be the first to throw a stone at her." Then He went back to writing in the dust.

One by one, the men put down their stones and walked away—beginning with the oldest all the way to the youngest. Finally, only the woman remained. Jesus asked her, "Woman, where are they? Has no one condemned you?" She said, "No one, sir." Then Jesus said to her, "Neither do I condemn you. Go now and leave your life of sin." (You can read about this in John 8:1–11.)

Jesus doesn't seek to condemn us. He isn't just waiting for us to sin so He can pounce on us and punish us. No! He *wants* us to leave our sin and accept God's forgiveness and move forward in our lives, doing what God commands and fulfilling what God holds out to us as His purpose for our life.

The Bible says, "This is good and acceptable in the sight of God our Savior, who desires all men to be saved and to come to the knowledge of the truth." (1 Tim. 2:3-4)

The Bible also says, "For God did not send His Son into the world to condemn the world, but that the world through Him might be saved." (John 3:17)

HOW TO GET INTO RIGHT RELATIONSHIP WITH GOD

At the time my wife and I moved to Houston, the Houston Oilers football team had a coach by the name of Bum Phillips. In many ways, he was the Mark Twain and Will Rogers of the NFL. In the late 1970s and early 1980s, Bum's Oilers were a good team. They may very well have gone to the Super Bowl twice if it hadn't been for the Pittsburgh Steelers standing in their way!

Over the years, Bum became a great friend. I saw him not long ago and was thrilled to hear that as a man in his seventies, he had accepted Christ as his Savior. He told me that no one had ever told him prior to that what he needed to do to be saved.

In case you are like my friend Bum, I want you to know how to be saved.

The Bible tells a story about a man named Nicodemus, who was a member of the Jewish ruling council. Most of the religious leaders called Pharisees were highly critical of Jesus because He preached about God's love, without requiring they keep a lot of the manmade rules that had evolved over the years. Nicodemus was a Pharisee, but he had an open curiosity and interest in Jesus. He came to Jesus at night because he didn't want everybody to see him going to the place where Jesus was staying. He also knew that this was a customary time for godly people to read and study the Law, so anyone who did see him going to visit Jesus might assume he was going to read the Scriptures with Him.

Nicodemus said to Jesus, "Rabbi, we know You are a teacher who has come from God. For no one could perform the miraculous signs You are doing if God were not with him."

Jesus replied to Nicodemus, "I tell you the truth, no one can see the kingdom of God unless he is born again."

Being "born again" and "being saved" are virtually interchangeable terms.

Nicodemus asked, "How can a man be born when he is old? Surely he cannot enter a second time into his mother's womb to be born!"

Jesus answered, "I tell you the truth, no one can enter the kingdom of God unless he is born of water and the Spirit. Flesh gives birth to flesh, but the Spirit gives birth to spirit."

As I shared in an earlier chapter, a few weeks after I accepted Jesus as my Savior, I was baptized. John the Baptist baptized Jesus. Being immersed in water was and is considered a sign of repentance. It is a powerful sign that we are putting off our old sinful nature—and that we are putting ourselves into a position to be thoroughly cleansed of our sin by God. When Jesus told Nicodemus that a spiritual birth happened by "water and the Spirit" He was referring to these waters of baptism. They are the outward and visible sign of a person who is sorry for sin and desires to be forgiven of it.

When Jesus referred to a spiritual birth happening by "the Spirit," He was referring to the fact that it is the Holy Spirit of God who changes our hearts and does the forgiving. It is the Holy Spirit who works in us and comes to dwell in us, enabling and empowering us to live a godly life.

Then Jesus told Nicodemus *how* a spiritual birth takes place. He said, "Just as Moses lifted up the snake in the desert, so the Son of Man must be lifted up, that everyone who believes in Him may have eternal life." In saying this, Jesus was referring to a story in the Old Testament. At one point in their wandering in the wilderness between Egypt and the Land of Promise, the Israelites sinned and a plague of poisonous snake bites broke out in their camp. God told Moses to make a bronze serpent and hang it on a pole. He then told Moses to tell the people that anyone who looked upon the bronze serpent would live and not die. That happened. (You can read all about it in Numbers 21:4–9.)

Jesus also was foretelling His own death on the cross. He knew He would be lifted up onto the cross and that He would hang there and die the death of crucifixion. And the good news was that anyone who looked on Him and believed that He was the sacrifice God had authorized to take away their sin…would be "saved" from eternal death and given eternal life!

The very next verse in this encounter with Nicodemus is perhaps the most famous statement in the entire New Testament. Jesus said, "For God so loved the world that He gave His only begotten Son, that whoever believes in Him should not perish but have everlasting life." (See John 3:1–16.)

Later, a man named Paul wrote to the Christians in Rome, "If you confess with your mouth the Lord Jesus and believe in your heart that God has raised Him from the dead, you will be saved." (Rom. 10:9) He reminded the Romans that God's Word says, "Whoever believes on Him will not be put to shame." (Rom. 10:11; see also Is. 28:16)

Being saved is a matter of believing that Jesus was the Son of God, that Jesus died on a cross as the sacrifice God required for sin, and that His dying in your place assures you of eternal life and a relationship with God, your heavenly Father, forever. Being saved means facing up to the fact that you have a sin nature—an inborn compulsion to sin—and that you are separated from God by your sin. It means admitting these facts to God and saying, "I am a sinner. I confess to You that I have lived in a way that is contrary to Your plan and purpose for my life. I ask You to forgive me of my sins and change my nature so that I will want to do what is right in Your eyes. Please accept me as Your child and give me the strength and courage to turn from my sin and follow Jesus as my Lord, obeying all that He taught and commanded."

The Bible says that when you do this, God immediately forgives you, accepts you, and gives you His own Holy Spirit to empower you to say "no" to sin and "yes" to God's ways. The Bible says, "If we confess our sins, He is faithful and just to forgive us our sins and to cleanse us from all unrighteousness." (1 John 1:9) The Bible also says:

> There is therefore now no condemnation to those who are in Christ Jesus, who do not walk according to the flesh, but according to the Spirit. For the law of the Spirit of life in Christ Jesus has made me free from the law of sin and death....
>
> For those who live according to the flesh set their minds on the things of the flesh, but those who live according to the Spirit, the things of the Spirit. For to be carnally minded is death, but to be spiritually minded is life and peace. Because the carnal mind is enmity against God; for it is not subject to the law of God, nor indeed can be. So then, those who are in the flesh cannot please God.
>
> But you are not in the flesh, but in the Spirit, if indeed the Spirit of God dwells in you. (Rom. 8:1–2, 5–9)

That's great news!

All God asks of us is that we *believe* in Jesus and *receive* what Jesus did on the cross as being for us personally. Being saved is not a matter of chalking up a long list of good deeds. It is solely a matter of believing and receiving.

So many people try to make salvation a long and complicated process, with lots of rules and steps. The Bible says, however, that the process is a very simple one…but a profound one. God Himself made the plan. He is the one who changes the human heart. Our part is simply to accept His plan and ask Him to do His work in us.

BEING GOOD ISN'T ENOUGH

Work your way to heaven?

Give your way to heaven?

Strive to be a "good enough person" to get to heaven?

The Bible says none of these ways works. Good deeds, good contributions, and good character don't count when it comes to being saved.

The Bible says, "For by grace you have been saved through faith, and that not of yourselves; it is the gift of God, not of works, lest anyone should boast." (Eph. 2:8–9)

Faith is what counts. And then faith, when it becomes active, produces good works. Faith is the engine that drives good works. Good works are never a substitute for faith. Our works don't get us into heaven—rather, they help point other people toward Christ. That's their purpose, not to bring us closer to God, but rather, to influence others to seek God. Faith-driven works extend or expand God's kingdom.

JESUS IS
THE ONLY "WAY"
TO THE FATHER

The only way to get to heaven and live in eternity is through faith in Jesus Christ as the Son of God. Let me repeat that: The *only* way to get to heaven and live in eternity is through faith in Jesus Christ as the Son of God.

The Bible is very clear on this point. You must have faith in *Jesus Christ*. The Bible says, "Nor is there salvation in any other, for there is no other name under heaven given among men by which we must be saved." (Acts 4:12) The Bible also says, "For God so loved the world that He gave His only begotten Son, that whoever believes in Him should not perish but have everlasting life." (John 3:16)

I've wondered at times how it is that Christians always seem to end up sitting in the good seats behind goals and behind the players' benches so they can show a John 3:16 sign on television. Is there a specific angel that transforms itself into various fans, traveling from stadium to stadium as a sign-toting witness? Or do dedicated Christians who love sports purposefully seek out these seats? Whatever the reason, I think this is one of the more fascinating ways that God communicates to us in today's culture.

In one of my favorite passages of the New Testament, Jesus said, "Enter by the narrow gate; for wide is the gate and broad is the way that leads to destruction, and there are many who go in by it. Because narrow is the gate and difficult is the way which leads to life, and there are few who find it." (Matt. 7:13–14) Jesus also said, "I am the door. If anyone enters by Me, he will be saved." (John 10:9)

THE RIGHT PERSPECTIVE ON GOOD WORKS

You may be saying, "But what, Dan, is the purpose for good deeds, good contributions, and good character?"

These things are a matter of REWARD to the person who has put his or her faith in Jesus Christ and is saved. These things don't get you into heaven, but they do impact the reward you will receive in eternity. They also determine the degree to which God will bless you on this earth prior to your dying and going to heaven.

The apostle Paul wrote to the Philippians, who had sent a material, very likely a financial, gift for his care while he was in prison. He thanked them for their gift and said, "You have done well that you shared in my distress." (Phil. 4:14) He went on to say, "Not that I seek the gift, but I seek the fruit that abounds to your account. Indeed, I have all and abound. I am full, having received from Epaphroditus the things which were sent from you, a sweet-smelling aroma, an acceptable sacrifice, well pleasing to God." (Phil. 4:17–18) He was referring to their account in God's reward system. Our good deeds, contributions, and godly character put us into position to receive an outpouring of supply from the Lord. Paul also wrote, "My God shall supply all your need according to His riches in glory by Christ Jesus." (Phil. 4:19)

MY CHALLENGE TO YOU: ACCEPT CHRIST TODAY

If you haven't already done so, I urge you to turn your *entire* life over to God. The prayer of salvation is such an easy one to pray. You can choose your own words but the basic prayer for any person who has never received Jesus as their Savior is this:

> Lord, I am a sinner. I know I am not in right standing with You, but I sincerely want to be. I believe that Jesus Christ died on the cross for me. I invite Him into my heart and from this day forward, I surrender all that I am and all that I have to Him. Please forgive me of all my sins. Help me to turn away from my sinful past and to live in the way You desire for me to live.

The Bible promises that "whoever calls upon the name of the LORD shall be saved." (Rom. 10:13)

If you pray a prayer such as this one with humility and a sincere heart, you *will* be forgiven and accepted as God's own beloved child, and you will have secured an eternal home in heaven. You will have done what God commanded—you will have expressed your belief in His only begotten Son, Jesus Christ. Even though you will die physically one day, your spirit and your identity will *never perish* eternally. You will live forever with the Lord.

8

BENEFIT #2

KNOWING WHY YOU ARE HERE ON EARTH

In the 1992 presidential debates, Ross Perot's vice-presidential running mate, Admiral Stockdale, asked the audience, "You may be wondering, who am I and why am I here?"

He was using that question as a rhetorical device. It is a question, however, that every adult person I know has asked himself or herself at some point, and not just in a philosophy class.

Have *you* ever wondered why you are on this earth?

There are moments in every life, I suspect, in which a person finds himself asking at some level, "Why am I alive on the earth? Is there any purpose in all this?"

The Bible says there is a plan and purpose for your life, and that God had it in mind long before you were born. Furthermore, the Bible says that you can discover that plan. The Bible says:

> I know the thoughts that I think toward you, says the LORD, thoughts of peace and not of evil, to give you a future and a hope. Then you will call upon Me and go and pray to Me, and I will listen to you. And you will seek Me and find Me, when you search for Me with all your heart. (Jer. 29:11–13)

It took me a while to discover God's plan for my life. It took me a while to discover the talents and skills that God had built into me as a human being.

I should perhaps make it VERY clear at this point that I am NOT the Dan Patrick who is a sportscaster on ESPN. He's younger, more talented, and better looking. Part of knowing your purpose in life is knowing who you are NOT. I am not *that* Dan Patrick. There are many other things I am not.

As a student and then as a young person pursuing career goals, I became very aware that I am a person of average abilities. In many areas of my life I probably am below average. Trust me, you certainly wouldn't want me to fix anything on your car or in your home. And you wouldn't want me to cook dinner for you. I totally missed out on those gifts from God.

Let me share a story with you. Many years ago my son and I undertook a Boy Scout project to bake a cake. I told my wife I thought I could handle making a simple bundt cake and smearing it with some icing. A few hours later she returned to the kitchen and saw me staring through the glass door of the oven. She asked me what I was doing. I told her I was waiting for the toothpick to pop out. She asked, "What toothpick?" I said, "The toothpick in the mix. It says on the box that the cake is done when the toothpick comes out clean."

After she stopped laughing, which was several minutes later, she explained to me what the instructions meant. No...I'm *not* a gourmet cook.

I was an average student in high school and college. Fortunately, I've always had some street smarts and common sense. I've also been willing to work as many hours as it took to get a job done and reach the next level, no matter what job I was doing at the time.

Like most people, I've had my share of bad times and good times, and a few pretty wild swings between my ups and downs. The fact that I'm writing a book is truly a miracle. I am grateful for the abundance of blessings God has poured out on me, an "average guy."

I'm not at all reluctant or dismayed to say that I'm an average guy. I take comfort in the fact that throughout history— and certainly from cover to cover in the Bible—God has chosen *average* men to do His bidding and convey His message. Abraham, Moses, and the disciples of Jesus considered themselves to be average men and questioned why they were chosen to do God's work.

When God spoke to Moses out of a burning bush that was alight with fire but was not consumed, Moses asked, "Who am I, that I should go to the Pharaoh, and that I should bring the children of Israel out of Egypt?" (Ex. 3:11) As his conversation with God unfolded, Moses questioned everything God commanded him to do. He was sure God must have chosen the wrong man. After all, he had a stuttering problem—how could he possibly be the speaker God needed him to be. He said to the Lord, "O my Lord, I am not eloquent, neither before nor since You have spoken to Your servant; but I am slow of speech and slow of tongue." (Ex. 4:10) He even begged for God to pick someone else for the job: "O my Lord, please send by the hand of whomever else You may send." (Ex. 4:13)

I've had that feeling. In the course of my career, I have been called upon a number of times to give speeches or sermons. I enjoy speaking to live audiences, but I also know that I am totally reliant upon God to help me in this area.

As I have trusted God, I *have* seen God's handiwork in the world and in my life. No bushes around my house have caught on fire, but I *have* felt God's presence. He *has* changed my heart. I also believe I actually heard His voice, very briefly one morning, arousing me out of a deep sleep so I wouldn't miss a church breakfast speech I was scheduled to deliver. Maybe it was just a low-ranking angel with wake-up-call duty. All I know with certainty is that if I had not heard that voice, I would have overslept and missed giving my talk.

That particular church message stands out in my mind, not only because of the voice I heard prior to giving it, but because of what happened afterward. A judge approached me and told me that he was not a believer and didn't know why he had attended the breakfast meeting. He shared with me that he was under severe stress and was struggling in his life. He said his wife had encouraged him to come to the meeting and then he told me that my message had changed his life. I assured him that it was not *my* message, but rather God speaking to him through me.

I left that encounter feeling very convinced that God had not wanted the judge to miss his appointment with God, and that I had been used specifically by God to deliver His message to the judge that day.

Yes, I'm just an average guy.

But I'm an average guy who is a sinner saved by grace.

And that's the main point of this chapter. My number-one REASON for being alive on the earth today is to be a Christian, a sinner saved by grace. I believe that is the number-one REASON God has for every person to be alive on the earth today. Accepting Jesus as your Savior and then leading others to Christ through your words and your works are the two primary things you are expected to do in your life. Everything else is secondary.

SEED SCATTERERS, NOT SEED GROWERS

For the first twenty-nine years of my life, I was just a sinner. And although I was baptized at age twenty-nine, it wasn't until I was forty-four that I fully committed my life to serving God. At that point, my "pre-season" as a Christian ended and I truly entered a time in my life when I was able to see a FULLNESS in God's plan and purpose for my being on the earth.

When I look back over my life, I know I always had a heart for the Lord. Sometimes I just didn't have the brain to go with it. The Bible says, "God knows your hearts." (Luke 16:15) God knows our motives, our intentions, our desires, our thoughts, our opinions, our creative ideas, our dreams. It is our challenge to discover these things about ourselves. It is up to us to discover the *greater* purpose God has for us.

Certainly I had a purpose in being a husband. I had a purpose in being a father. I had a purpose in being a member of a church. I had a purpose in being a quality broadcaster bringing people accurate information. But after I accepted Jesus Christ as my Savior, I took on a still higher or greater purpose. I became a "seed scatterer" for God's garden.

I see myself today as planting seeds in people's lives. I'm not in the heart-changing business. Only God can cause the seed of an idea or the seeds embodied by words to take root and grow. Only God can change a heart. He is the Master Sower who is capable of tilling the soil of our lives and bringing forth a harvest. I'm just a seed-scatterer, but it is the most important and exciting job I've ever had!

The Bible says that many people are like ripe fruit or grain—they are ready to hear the message of God and accept it. Jesus said to His disciples, "The harvest truly is plentiful, but the laborers are few. Therefore pray the Lord of the harvest to send out laborers into His harvest." (Matt 9:37–38)

Every person who accepts Christ is expected to scatter seeds. These might be in the form of words...or deeds...or contributions... or prayer...or all of the above. All forms of ministry and benevolence become seeds that God can grow as *He* desires.

What is our part?

I believe God expects us to find out what we are good at doing, and then do that in a way that brings honor to Him, gets out His Word of salvation, and brings practical and spiritual help to others. From cover to cover the Bible has verses that expressly outline these activities for the believer. I challenge you to find them, read them, and apply them to your specific life.

Here are a few verses to get you started:

- Mark 5:19–20

- Matthew 28:19–20

- 1 Corinthians 3:5–9

- Mark 4:1–20

- Romans 12:1–8

If you *want* to get to a point in your life where you know you are doing *precisely* what God created you to do and desires for you to do, then I can't urge you strongly enough to open your Bible and spend some quiet time in God's Word. Again, let me recommend the books of Matthew and John to you. Read the book of Psalms. Read Proverbs. A major reason for your being on the earth is so that you will DO what these books tell you to do!

THERE IS ONLY ONE YOU

When it comes to your individual talents and abilities…

If you are musically inclined, God expects you to become a good musician and to use your talent for the Lord.

If you are great with children, God expects you to get involved with children in some way and train them up to serve God.

If you are skilled in words, God expects you to develop your talents as a writer and use those talents in spreading the Gospel and encouraging Christians in many walks of life.

For every set of talents and skills, God has a purpose of ministry. He has a way for you to "scatter seeds" of the Gospel that He can turn into a harvest.

IT'S NOT A QUESTION OF FORTUNE OR FAME

Although I work in television and radio, I don't consider myself a celebrity. I'm nobody special. Few people outside of Houston, and a lot of people *in* Houston, have never heard of me. Even if I had a high-profile network job, I would not consider myself anyone special.

One of the things my job has allowed me to do is to interview people who *are* celebrities, many of whom are not only famous, but rich.

The one conclusion I have taken away from these encounters is that real joy and fulfillment are not dependent on fame, fortune, or power. I've met a number of rich and famous people who are miserable. Their priorities are all wrong. They've factored God out. They have very little sense of personal fulfillment or satisfaction.

Very few people know, for example, that when Elvis Presley died he was reading a book about Jesus. According to his close friend Joe Esposito—as told on *Larry King Live*—Joe was the first to find Elvis dead in Elvis' bathroom. Elvis was clutching a book titled *The Shroud of Turin*, which is a book about the burial cloth that many believed covered the body of Jesus after He was laid in the tomb.

To the outside world, Elvis had it all. The truth was that Elvis lived a tortured, unhappy life hooked on booze, drugs, and women. He was known to love gospel music and recorded many gospel albums. He was known to attend church. His lifestyle, however, was not that of a person committed to the Lord. In his final days, knowing he was very ill, even the King of Rock and Roll had apparently figured out that what he had lived for in his life—fame and fortune—were not the answers to genuine happiness and peace. When the curtain came down on Elvis for the last time he was searching for Jesus.

In contrast, some of the happiest people I have met are people who had very little in the way of material possessions, recognition, or status. They were people who have accepted Jesus Christ as their personal Savior and are believing, applying, and living out the Bible in their own little worlds—which, by the way, they have turned into a little bit of heaven on earth.

Our purpose for being on this earth is not to earn great amounts of money, to become nationally famous, or to rule an empire. Our purpose is to love and serve the Lord in the place He has put us and with all the gifts and talents He has given us.

Don't Worry about the "Importance" of Your Work. If you stack up jobs that are truly "important" in our world, being in the media would be closer to the bottom than to the top. I suspect in many people's minds, we in the media are like politicians and lawyers. We talk a lot but don't produce much in the way of real goods and services. If you happen to be a politician, lawyer, or fellow member of the media…you know I'm right! If you are a teacher, physician, farmer, policeman, fireman, nurse, member of the clergy, community volunteer, or serve in our military, your careers are far more important than that of any media person I know.

If you are a truck driver keeping America's shelves stocked, a construction worker building our nation, a researcher finding tomorrow's answers to today's problems, a small business owner creating jobs, or a janitor keeping our offices sanitary for another day's work … you are doing important work!

If you are a stay-at-home mother—making personal, financial, and career sacrifices to raise your children "full-time"—you are doing *very important work*. If you are a grandparent who has taken on the role of raising your grandchildren, you too are doing *very important* work!

The fact is, we are all important to the process of making this world work and making America the great nation it is. You've heard of the food chain. In our careers, we're a "people chain." We each have a place. All jobs are important to God!

The Bible says we are called to be accountable according to our gifts from God. We are to *use* what we have been given. Jesus told a great parable about this. He said:

> For the kingdom of heaven is like a man traveling to a far country, who called his own servants and delivered his goods to them. And to one he gave five talents, to another two, and to another one, to each according to his own ability; and immediately he went on a journey. Then he who had received the five talents went and traded with them, and made another five talents. And likewise he who had received two gained two more also. But he who had received one went and dug in the ground, and hid his lord's money. After a long time the lord of those servants came and settled accounts with them.

So he who had received five talents came and brought five other talents, saying, "Lord, you delivered to me five talents; look, I have gained five more talents besides them." His lord said to him, "Well done, good and faithful servant; you were faithful over a few things, I will make you ruler over many things. Enter into the joy of your lord." He also who had received two talents came and said, "Lord, you delivered to me two talents; look, I have gained two more talents besides them." His lord said to him, "Well done, good and faithful servant; you have been faithful over a few things. I will make you ruler over many things. Enter into the joy of your lord."

Then he who had received the one talent came and said, "Lord, I knew you to be a hard man, reaping where you have not sown, and gathering where you have not scattered seed. And I was afraid, and went and hid your talent in the ground. Look, there you have what is yours."

But his lord answered and said to him, "You wicked and lazy servant, you knew that I reap where I have not sown, and gather where I have not scattered seed. So you ought to have deposited my money with the bankers, and at my coming I would have received back my own with interest. Therefore take the talent from him, and give it to him who has ten talents." (Matt. 25:14–28)

"Wow," you may be saying, "that seems pretty harsh." Jesus was showing how very serious the Lord is about our USE of what He entrusts to us.

The good news is that every person who willfully and eagerly "used" or "invested" the talents and abilities God has given to him will experience a doubling of those talents and abilities...and will receive praise from God for doing so! I have seen this biblical principle work time and time again in people's lives. It has worked in my life.

It is the person who does NOT use any of his or her God-given talents and abilities who finds that he is unproductive, unrewarded, and in the end, miserable.

In this story, the man who buried his one talent makes a terrible false claim. He says that the Master is a hard man who harvests where he hasn't sown, and gathers where he hasn't scattered seed.

How many people do you know who have that opinion of God? They see Him as a harsh judge, not a loving Father. They see Him as demanding and requiring things that man doesn't have to give, and that He expects us to do what we cannot do.

Nothing could be further from the truth!

God is not "hard"—He is generous, patient, kind, and loving. He has the very same attributes as Jesus. Indeed, He bears the attributes that are described for us as the "fruit" of the Holy Spirit—meaning the *nature* of the Holy Spirit. God's character is one of love, joy, peace, patience, kindness, goodness, faithfulness, gentleness, and self-control. (See Gal. 5:22.) (When people speak of the "fruit of the Spirit" these are the character traits they mean.)

God doesn't ask us to be something He is not. To the contrary, He says in filling us with His very own Holy Spirit, He enables us to become like He is!

Furthermore, God doesn't harvest where He hasn't sown. He harvests where He *has* sown. He has sown many things into your life. He has given you breath and life and energy and talent and opportunity and associations and relationships. Above all, He has given you His Spirit. Acknowledge that all you have and all that is good in nature are things that God has given to you!

Don't worry about what others have. What have *you* been given? What have *you* done with your gifts and God-given talents?

Accept Jesus as your Savior and then serve Him with the abilities you have been given ... and you *will* know your reason for being on this earth!

9

BENEFIT #3

RECEIVING GOD'S DAILY GUIDANCE

After I had accepted Jesus as my Savior and had been baptized at age twenty-nine, I was very excited about my new faith and my new life. I truly *felt* born again!

As I stated earlier, the problem was that I didn't follow up and live in the way that I knew God wanted me to live.

The long and short of it is that I talked a good game but I didn't walk the talk. It is fairly common knowledge among pastors of churches that out of every ten people who join a church and say they have accepted Jesus as their Savior, about half stop coming to church within a year. I was one of those who fell away.

Oh, I was still interested in the Bible but I didn't read it regularly and I wasn't involved in a Bible study class. I still loved Jesus, but I didn't attend church regularly.

Because I was a television personality and publicity had circulated that I had accepted Jesus as my Savior, I was invited to speak to church groups. I accepted because I was too embarrassed to say "no." Also, I didn't want to let God down. The fact is, I *should* have said "no." I wasn't remotely ready to speak and I was still clueless about the Word of God.

As far as I am concerned, some churches make a huge mistake in asking brand-new Christians to speak. They aren't prepared. The end result is often embarrassing for both the speaker and the audience.

Just about a year ago, I was asked to give a Sunday sermon by my pastor, Dr. Ed Young. I've been on radio and television for twenty years, but giving that sermon in front of an audience was the toughest thing I have ever done. There were almost 4,000 people in church that day. I knew many of them personally and I knew that many people in that church building knew a lot more about the Bible than I knew. I was afraid I'd make a major mistake. I tried to lighten the moment by telling them I was teaching from the book of Galileo. Some in the crowd laughed. But others, I think, believed that I truly thought there was a book by that name in the Bible. There isn't.

One thing that brings me some comfort is that I am far more prepared today to speak about the Bible in public than I was twenty years ago, or even five years ago. I readily admit, however, that I still have much to learn.

And the fact is, so do you. No matter how long you have known Jesus as your Savior and no matter how many years you have read and studied the Bible, you, too, still have much to learn! There is never an ending point to our learning from the Bible. There's always more that God has to say to us through His Word.

A Spiritual Book that Has Increased Meaning as You Grow

I say all that to say this. The Bible is a spiritual book and because of that, it has a truly amazing quality to it. Every time you read the Bible, it speaks to you as if you are reading it for the first time.

How can that be? Two main reasons. First, the more you read the Bible regularly, the more you begin to see connections among various passages. You begin to have new insights into the meaning of the Bible because you suddenly recall how something Jesus said relates to an Old Testament story, or how a story in the Bible is linked to a commandment or a promise of God.

Second, the longer you love the Lord and seek to follow Him closely—praying regularly and growing in your relationship with Him—the more you mature in your faith. The more you mature in your relationship with the Lord, the more ways you see to apply God's Word to your daily life and experiences. Plus, just in the normal process of aging, you find that you have different experiences that NEED an application of God's Word!

Therefore, each time you come to the Bible to read a particular passage, you simply aren't the same person you were the last time you read that passage! You have changed in ways that allow you to have greater understanding about what you read.

The bottom line to all this is that the more you learn about God's Word, the more He reveals to you how to use His Word, and along the way, the more your appreciation for and reliance upon the Word of God grows!

As we trust God day by day, He provides for us exactly what we need THAT DAY.

STAYING YOKED UP WITH GOD'S WORD

Jesus said, "Come to Me, all you who labor and are heavy laden, and I will give you rest. Take My yoke upon you and learn from Me, for I am gentle and lowly in heart, and you will find rest for your souls. For My yoke is easy and My burden is light." (Matt. 11:28–30)

A yoke is a heavy wooden harness. When oxen and other beasts of burden are yoked together, they become very useful for pulling carts, plows, and wagons. To an ox, however, a yoke is *not* heavy if it has been designed to fit perfectly the contours of the ox. The burden being pulled or the work being done is not difficult if the yoke fits, and if the other ox in the yoke is pulling his weight.

What Jesus promises us is that He will give us a yoke that fits us perfectly—He promises that He will put us into work and into a ministry seed-scattering role that is perfectly suited to our inborn talents, abilities, and desires. Furthermore, He is yoked with us. He is in partnership with us, helping us. He pulls far more than His fair share of the load!

Yokes do two things—they guide a team of work animals along a straight path in the line they are to walk. And, they allow the animals to do meaningful and purposeful work. The same for us! When we are yoked up with Jesus, He keeps us walking in a straight path that is in full obedience to God's Word. He gives us purposeful and fulfilling and meaningful tasks to do—assignments that give us joy and satisfaction beyond measure!

Jesus not only promises us eternal life, He promises us an abundant life until the day we die. Jesus said, "The thief [referring to the devil] does not come except to steal, and to kill, and to destroy. I have come that they may have life, and that they may have it more abundantly." (John 10:10)

The guidance that God gives us daily is guidance that leads us from blessing to blessing and from strength to strength. We grow as we obey and see God's work done in us, through us, and all around us. We produce *good* fruit. We exhibit godly behavior. We enter into a life of genuine purpose and fulfillment. We experience an *abundant* life!

How God Guided Me to Write this Book

Let me give you a practical example of this from my own life. Early in the book I told you why I titled this book the way I did. There is more to the story.

A few years ago I was vacationing with my family. As had become my custom the last few years, I took my Bible with me, as well as a couple of Bible-related audiotapes and books. I usually spend the vast majority of a vacation having fun with my family and friends, but I also like to have a quiet part of every vacation to read and revive the inner me. Some people read magazines or novels to unwind and refresh their minds and emotions. I read God's Word.

On this particular vacation, I was spending quiet time with God one afternoon just before dinner. I like the verse in the Bible that says, "Be still, and know that I am God." (Ps. 46:10) I prayed that God would show me how I might better serve Him here on earth.

I had already come to the point in my life's journey in which I had put God first in my life. I had been doing everything I knew to do: be a godly husband and father, try to be a good Christian witness in the workplace, support my church and other Christian causes with my time, talent, and financial gifts, and give money to help with Bible translation work. But now I wanted to do more.

Please don't misunderstand my intent. I wasn't trying to come up with a plan to make up for past sins or earn extra credit in heaven. I just wanted to do more to serve God than I was presently doing.

As I asked the Lord for guidance, instantly I felt impressed to write a book titled *The Second Most Important Book You'll Ever Read.* Rarely does God answer my prayers so quickly, or so definitively. I have never written a book before, but it became very clear to me that God could use even an average person to write a simple book about the joys and benefits of reading the Bible. So here I am. And here you are.

I went to dinner that night and announced to my family that I was going to write a book. That was several years ago.

Although God had given me a plan of action, He hadn't told me WHEN to write this book. I knew enough to know that God not only tells us what to do, but He tells us when to act. I needed to wait. Looking back, I can see that I wasn't prepared to write this book at that time. I needed to do a lot more reading, a lot more study, and a lot more listening to God before I sat down at my computer.

Over the years since that time, I have waited patiently for God to say, "Now is the time."

GREEN LIGHTS AND RED LIGHTS

I strongly believe in a green-light, red-light approach to life. Before I factored God into my life and became a committed

Christian, I made decisions based on what I thought was the right course of action at any given time. I never asked for God's direction. I thought I knew best … or at least could figure out with my own mind what was best. It never really dawned on me that God might have an opinion—and that His opinion might be the only one that counted!

Does that sound like a familiar pattern?

There were times, of course, when I saw a red light, but I chose to run right through it as if it were green because I wanted to do what *I* wanted to do! I acted on *my* desires, *my* wishes, *my* goals, even if all logic, reason, and plain ol' common sense were stacked against my decisions.

Let me assure you, there were a number of broadside collisions in my life. I was just an accident waiting to happen.

Most people I know have done things that an inner voice was telling them not to do. I include myself in that group. How about you? I'm not only talking about decisions that lead to sin. I'm talking also about major life decisions concerning marriage, career, financial investments, and other important areas of life about which we make decisions every day.

For the past several years, I have not made a major decision without getting a green light from God. I always ask Him for guidance. If I am not absolutely sure in my heart that I am going down the path the Lord wants me to travel, I don't go.

How do I know when the light is green?

Trust me, when you have chosen God as your Master, you know. Some may call it an inner voice. Others may call it a strong urging or prompting in the spirit. Still others might call it a sharp pang of conscience.

GETTING A
GREEN LIGHT FROM GOD

It took about three years before God gave me the green light for writing this book. He gave me the concepts I should present to you and the plan for publishing and marketing this book.

I am told that there are almost 100,000 books written in the United States every year. Most of those books are never read except by the author's family members and friends. So why do I have feelings of peace and confidence as I write? Because I have a strong assurance that God is in charge. If *you* are the *only* person to read this book, then so be it. God must really have wanted to speak to you! If God wants to reach thousands of people, or just you, that is alright with me. I have learned that when I partner up with God, I need to be prepared for GOOD things to happen, and sometimes those good things are also GREAT things.

I don't know what God has planned next for me. I have a strong confidence that whatever it is, it will be good for God and good for me. Knowing that God has my eternal good and earthly blessing at the heart of His desire for me gives me great excitement. It gives life meaning.

I claim as my theme song a statement that the apostle Paul wrote to the church at Philippi: "I can do all things through Christ who strengthens me." (Phil. 4:13)

If you haven't trusted God in this way in your personal life, let me assure you that there is a tremendous sense of peace in knowing that you are precisely where God wants you to be. There is a feeling of comfort, even in troubling moments. In fact, the Bible teaches that even in times of trouble, we should rejoice, knowing that God is working in our lives.

10

BENEFIT #4

GETTING THROUGH TOUGH TIMES WITH GOD

The Bible has a number of stories that illustrate this great truth: God uses our problems to teach us valuable lessons or as a means of disciplining us so we will remove certain things from our lives or adopt new spiritual habits. He teaches us and disciplines us as loving Father, always with our *best* outcome in mind. The Bible says, "My son, do not despise the chastening of the LORD, nor detest His correction; for whom the LORD loves He corrects, just as father the son in whom he delights." (Prov. 3:11–12)

I experienced this in my own life.

Two things happened in 1984 that impacted the rest of my life. My daughter Shane was born. And, I decided that I was ready to move on to a new career. I decided I didn't want to spend the rest of my life giving ball scores every night on television. I had lived that dream for almost seven years.

I don't know if this has happened to you, but I found that getting what I wanted hadn't brought me the complete and total happiness I thought it would. There are few things more frustrating than having your dreams come true, and then finding that your dream doesn't make you happy. What do you do next?

During my years as a sportscaster I had interviewed a number of professional athletes. They seemed to fall into two groups. The larger group seemed restless and unhappy. The smaller group seemed happy and at peace. I discovered that the larger group thought that they would be very happy living out their childhood dream of being a major league player. They had found, however, that happiness eluded them. I personally believe this is why many athletes, celebrities, politicians, and high-profile businessmen abuse alcohol, drugs, and women. They never have enough to make themselves "happy." They believe if they only can get a little more of something that gives them physical pleasure, they'll be happy.

The Bible teaches that if a person builds his or her life around a career, money, power, or possessions, that person will always be disappointed. The Bible asks, "What is a man profited if he gains the whole world, and loses his own soul? Or what will a man give in exchange for his soul?" (Matt. 16:26)

Jesus taught, "Do not lay up for yourselves treasures on earth, where moth and rust destroy and where thieves break in and steal; but lay up for yourselves treasures in heaven, where neither moth nor rust destroys and where thieves do not break in and steal. For where your treasure is, there your heart will be also." (Matt. 6:19–21)

Jesus also said, "No one can serve two masters; for either he will hate the one and love the other, or else he will be loyal to the one and despise the other. You cannot serve God and mammon." (Matt. 6:24)

The other much smaller group of athletes I observed had a different view of life. They were Christians who put God first. They viewed their career as simply a platform for their personal ministry. They were at peace because they had a personal relationship with Jesus Christ. They knew they had found the true meaning to life, and with it, eternal fulfillment, not mere temporary earthly happiness.

For the past several years I have been involved in my radio business and politics. Once again, I found two groups of people: a larger group pursuing money and power—a group never fulfilled personally—and a much smaller group focused on what is truly important in life, God and His plans and purposes.

In which group are you? In which group would you like to be? In which group *should* you be?

Pursuing a New Dream

In 1984 as I was seeking a new career, I decided to go into the restaurant and bar business. While hosting an afternoon television talk show about a year earlier, I had met a well-known restaurateur and that encounter had sparked my interest in that particular business. I was under the foolish impression that if I worked for myself I would have more free time. What a mistake that was! On top of that foolish notion, I entered one of the toughest industries in which to be successful, and it was a business I knew nothing about. (Remember my experience in baking a toothpick out of a cake!)

Within two years, I had become involved in five establishments. I had hundreds of employees and a huge in-over-my-head nightmare. The business threatened my health and my marriage. Then in 1986, the economy crashed in Houston. That year almost 1,200 restaurants closed in Houston, including four of my five establishments. The fifth restaurant barely kept its doors open, and that was because my mother and father worked for me in that location. Had they not been there, taking little or no pay, that location also would have closed.

By the end of the year I was forced to declare personal bankruptcy.

GRADUATING FROM THE UNIVERSITY OF BANKRUPTCY

In the early 1980s, Houston banks would loan a person a lot of money just on their name. Landlords would sign a person to a long lease with nothing more than a signature. No one saw the recession coming. Those old enough to remember may recall the bank and savings and loan crash in the mid-1980s. Besides those involved in fraud, many lenders and borrowers simply had overextended themselves thinking the good times would never end. We went through this same flawed logic in the stock market of the 1990s and the dot-com boom that went to bust.

I'll never forget the feeling I had in 1986. At age thirty-six, I was broke. I had given up my dream career in television. I had made poor business decisions. I had run through a lot of red lights. I had left God totally out of the equation. How could this happen to me? How could I ever recover?

I wasn't mad at God. I didn't blame Him. How could I? I never asked for His guidance. The decisions were mine.

As I now look back on that chapter in my life I view it as a learning experience. I didn't realize how God was working in my life at that very moment. He was preparing me for what was ahead. I like to think of that time as attending the University of Bankruptcy. The tuition was extremely high, but the education was priceless.

One of the great lessons I learned is that even when we get off track with God's plans and purposes for us … He has a "Plan B" that He is always ready to put into effect the moment we are willing to pursue it!

DON'T TOUCH THAT DIAL!

In May of 1988 I was still working in my one remaining restaurant. We were scraping by one day at a time. I knew I would probably have to go back into sales work. I had been out of television for almost four years and I had lost my contacts in that business. I didn't want to have to start over again in a small town.

One day, a face from out of the past came into the restaurant. I didn't really know him but I had seen him around the locker rooms. He had been a reporter for a small radio station. He asked me if I would be interested in doing a radio sports talk show for a station in Tomball, Texas, a little town about forty miles north of Houston. I had never heard of this station. It had only been on the air a year. They played big band music most of the day.

When this man first mentioned the job, I had an immediate feeling that the job was "far beneath me." After all, I had worked in Washington, D.C., with Al Roker. I had worked for a top television station in Houston. I had hired Jim Nance, now the number-one sportscaster with CBS. I had covered four Super Bowls, NBA Championships, and almost every big sporting event in the nation. I had interviewed almost every big name star in sports. Why, I had even been invited to the White House! How could I consider taking this job in Tomball, Texas?

I thought about the opportunity, however, and sized up my financial situation at the time, and decided I needed to push aside my pride and take the job. I didn't see this talk show as a way of resuming my broadcasting career, but as a way to save my restaurant. I decided I would build a little studio in my restaurant and bring in sports stars to attract new customers. The show might AIR out of Tomball, Texas, but it would originate in my place of business.

I built the studio. I did the show for a few weeks and it seemed to go well. Then one day I plugged in my equipment to connect with the station and no one at the station responded. It turned out the employees at that station had not been paid in months. The station owner owed the government for back taxes and bank loans were overdue. The owner's partners were suing him and he was suing them. I was staring headlong into another disaster! But out of disaster can also come opportunity. After a lot of persuasion, I convinced both sides to sell to me.

I only had one problem. I was broke and I needed *one million dollars* for the deal. I told my tale to one of my bar customers who said he might know someone interested in putting up the money. He set an appointment at the restaurant for the next day, and as luck would have it, that morning one of my key employees didn't show up for work. At the time the man arrived for the appointment, I was cleaning the restrooms—someone had to do it! I didn't have time to stop and talk, so for a few minutes while I was cleaning, I discussed my business plan with this total stranger. He listened and said he would get back to me. I frankly figured I'd never see him again. But, after lunch he called. He said he would put up whatever money I needed. I could hardly believe it!

Despite this incredible event, I failed to see God's hand working in my life.

WHAT'S A RUSH LIMBAUGH?

After several months we took control of the station. Our business plan was a very simple one: keep costs down and build up advertising revenues by turning the station over to a talk format. Our goal was to turn around the station and then sell it for a small profit as quickly as we could.

One day not long after we took over the station, a stranger called. He introduced himself as Rush Limbaugh. I thought to myself, *What kind of name is that*? He proceeded to tell me about himself and his new radio show. In those days Rush wasn't on major stations in big cities. He was broadcasting on smaller stations that could reach into the bigger-city markets. His show didn't cost us anything to air—all we had to do was give him a few commercials that he could sell to national clients. Not only was the price right, but I liked his show.

The old saying, "the rest is history"…became true! Within a few months our little station had higher ratings than some of the big stations in Houston. Rush had put us on everyone's radio dial. After a year or so the big stations all wanted his program. He could have left us, but he didn't. Rush was very loyal to those who had helped him when he needed help. And to this day, I appreciate what Rush did for us.

A few years later, in 1992, we had a chance to buy one of those *big* stations. By this time, however, my partner didn't have any additional money to invest. We tried to borrow money from forty-three different banks. All said "no." We were down to the last few days to complete the deal and get the loan. We still needed a little more money and all of my Houston sources were tapped out. I was given the phone number of a businessman in Atlanta who I was told might be interested in this kind of investment. I called him, and within twenty minutes, he agreed to put up the cash we needed. To this day, I have never met this man face to face. We only corresponded by phone and mail. Once again, I failed to see the hand of God in my life. I wasn't looking.

WHY DO
GOOD PEOPLE SUFFER?

Two of the questions that many people ask are: Why do people suffer? Why does God allow hard times, especially in the lives of those who seem to be innocent victims?

People I have met through the years have said to me, "Dan, I just can't understand how God allows bad things to happen to good people." Most people who ask this are especially concerned about the abuse and suffering of children.

As I sat down to address this question, two terrible stories were in the headlines. Major league pitcher Darryl Kile, a 33-year-old father of four young children, died of a heart attack. By all accounts, he was a fine human being, a loving husband and father.

The second headline story was about a bus crash involving a bus that was taking children to a church camp. The driver and several children were killed.

It was easy to ask, "Why, God?" in response to both stories.

Several years ago, the world was rocked by the death of professional golfer Payne Stewart. He regularly wore a WWJD (What Would Jesus Do) bracelet and was a standout Christian on a world stage. Why?

Just a little over a year ago now, our entire nation was rocked by the attacks that occurred on September 11, 2001. America lost nearly three thousand souls that day: wives, husbands, children, parents, rescue workers—all leaving families and loved ones to grieve. Why?

Almost every person I know has watched a beloved family member or friend suffer—perhaps in the past, perhaps right now. You may be suffering as you read these words.

Pastors have told me that more people turn to God during times of suffering than at any other time in their life. It is during suffering that we tend to feel we have lost control of our lives and that we have nowhere else to turn but to God.

Every time we see a national tragedy, we also see people turn to prayer and to meeting together in church services to honor and remember those who have been killed, wounded, or have suffered a loss. Churches begin to overflow and all-night prayer vigils seem to occur spontaneously. On the Sunday following the September 11 attacks, people were standing in the aisles and sitting on the floor at my church. At the end of the service, more people stepped forward indicating they were accepting Jesus Christ as their Savior than I had ever seen in a church service.

Does God purposely allow tragedy in people's lives or even create terrible times of suffering just so more people will turn to Him? The answer is "NO." God does, however, USE these times in our lives to draw us closer to Himself.

Let's take a little closer look at suffering. Suffering usually occurs in one of four categories: suffering caused by our own behavior, suffering caused by others who have inflicted pain upon us, suffering that occurs simply because we are in the wrong place at the wrong time, and suffering that is just plain ol' unexplainable.

Suffering Caused by Our Own Behavior

The sad but overwhelming fact is that the vast majority of the health problems that create suffering are caused by one or more of the following: what we eat, how much we eat, what we drink, how much we drink, smoking, the taking of harmful drugs, a dangerous sexual lifestyle, a failure to exercise, a failure to get proper medical attention, and the overuse of prescription drugs (including use of drugs that have dangerous interactions with one another). All of these are behaviors we can *control*.

God gives us the free will to live as we choose. Most people do not choose to live a healthy lifestyle. Over time, bad health habits can produce diseases that in turn, are marked by suffering.

In America, we seem to have perfected the art of denial. We overeat, drink too much, smoke, and don't exercise…and we always conclude that it's the "other guy" who is going to have a heart attack and develop cancer. We have been well-informed through a wide variety of sources about the harmful effects associated with those four main lifestyle factors, yet we continue as a nation to overeat, overdrink, smoke, and live totally sedentary lives. Christians are not spared from the ill effects that come from lifestyle choices.

Suffering Inflicted by Others

Suffering is not only a life and death issue. Many times people are mentally and sometimes physically injured by what other people do to them. Spouses, family members, friends, co-workers, employers, employees, and total strangers can hurt any one of us on any given day.

Once again, God has given mankind free will. Some people choose to exercise their free will and engage in evil acts. As long as evil exists in any person anywhere in the world, our world is subject to "random acts of violence."

Christians are not immune from being hurt, or from hurting others. We all are guilty at times of "trespassing" on the garden of another person's life—sometimes we do so unconsciously, at other times out of a burst of spite, revenge, anger, or mistrust. The call to the Christian is twofold:

First, when the Christian realizes he has hurt another person, he has the responsibility for asking forgiveness and making restitution.

Second, when a Christian is hurt by someone, he has the challenge to forgive first, refuse to hang on to the hurt, and to pray for the other person. Jesus taught this about the response His followers should make toward their persecutors: "Love your enemies, bless those who curse you, do good to those who hate you, and pray for those who spitefully use you and persecute you, that you may be sons of your Father in heaven." (Matt. 5:44–45)

Doing these two things may not remove us from all suffering at the hands of others, but it does allow us to respond to the suffering in a positive, godly manner. In the midst of suffering, there is great inner satisfaction that comes from knowing you are displaying God-approved character.

September 11, 2001, is a day America will never forget. It is a day when suffering was inflicted upon the innocent by outside forces. Among the nearly three thousand people who died that day were Todd Beamer and Tom McGuinness. Todd was a passenger on United Flight 93 and Tom was a pilot on American Flight 11.

Todd Beamer's last known words have now become famous: "Let's roll." Todd's wife, Lisa Beamer, is a Christian. She has been an incredible example of the power of God's Word to help sustain a person in unbelievably difficult times. She has been unwavering in her belief in God and has been a living testament to how faith gives a person hope and peace in the midst of intense grief.

Cheryl McGuinness, Tom's wife, has been another outstanding witness of how God can help a person through a terrible time of suffering. She was a recent guest on my radio program and I sat in amazement at her calm, steady confidence that God remains in full control of her life.

Watching and listening to these two women on various media programs has reaffirmed my belief that one of the outcomes of suffering can be a very strong witness to the sustaining power of faith in Jesus Christ. It seems that even in the most difficult circumstances, God raises up people out of the ashes of despair to share the good news of the Gospel. Their message is even more potent to the world because of the suffering and loss they have experienced. In some way, I believe Lisa and Cheryl have been "chosen" by God to be witnesses for Christ in this time. They are an example to all of us that as we trust God in our suffering, we can emerge stronger from a time of suffering, not weaker. God spoke this through the prophet Isaiah:

> "Behold, I have created the blacksmith
> Who blows the coals in the fire,
> Who brings forth an instrument for his work....
> This is the heritage of the servants of the LORD,
> And their righteousness is from Me," says the LORD.
> (Is. 54:16–17)

I see that verse being lived out by Lisa Beamer and Cheryl McGuinness.

Being in the Wrong Place at the Wrong Time

Sometimes we simply are in the wrong place at the wrong time. Accidents happen. People make mistakes. Machines break or malfunction unexpectedly. We could stop all traffic accidents if we all stopped driving vehicles. We could eliminate all air disasters if we grounded all airplanes. We could eliminate drowning if we just eliminated all water. I think you get the point.

Life has its dangers. We can do our best to avoid them, prepare for them, and avert them … but we cannot totally eliminate them.

Unexplainable Reasons

There are some root causes of suffering that are simply unexplainable. No one person or group is at "fault." Diseases exist for which there is no known cause or cure. Natural disasters and storms come without any means of human decision-making or control.

THE RIGHT QUESTIONS TO ASK IN HARD TIMES

The questions we must ask about each of these causes of suffering are these:

"Did God cause this?"

The answer from the Bible is NO. God does not purposefully hurt His people. God protects, provides, and causes His people to persevere, prevail, and prosper. That is the overriding message of the Bible from cover to cover. God *does* act to defeat those who would destroy His people. He moves against those who become *His* enemies. But God does not send tragedy and suffering into the lives of His children.

The Bible states that the enemy of our souls does this work. Jesus said, "The thief does not come except to steal, and to kill, and to destroy. I have come that they may have life, and that they may have it more abundantly." (John 10:10) It is the work of Satan to diminish, degrade, damage, and dent everything that God calls good and calls His own.

"Could God have prevented this?"

The answer from the Bible is YES. God has all power, wisdom, and presence. He can do anything He chooses to do. He knows everything—He is never taken by surprise by a tragedy. But God has chosen by His own mandate *NOT* to overstep the boundaries of self-imposed human will. He has chosen *NOT* to violate His natural physical laws, including laws related to disease—even if we do not yet fully understand all of those laws. He has chosen *NOT* to violate His own commandments and statutes and principles regarding human behavior.

There are countless reasons why God might choose not to intervene in stopping or lessening suffering. We simply don't know them all. That is one of the GREAT truths of the Bible: We are finite and God is infinite. We are the created beings and God is the Creator. We cannot see the ending or beginning of anything...He sees into eternity past and eternity future.

We also must face the fact that death comes to every person. Ever since Adam and Eve sinned in the Garden of Eden, a physical death has brought an end to a physical life.

When we are faced with all of the reasons for suffering and the reasons why God might not intervene in suffering, we are left with one great conclusion: God alone knows. Our trust in Him is what we call "faith." It is a matter of saying, "I do not have all the answers but I am connected to the One who does have the answers. I choose to trust in God."

A pastor once told me of a family that had virtually everything of a material nature that a family might want. They were major financial supporters of the church, and by all accounts were "good" people who volunteered their time and talents for the Lord on numerous occasions. One day, a drunk driver killed their only son, a teenager. They were devastated. They could hardly get through a day. Several months later they came to their pastor to tell him that they believed the loss of their son was the worst thing that could ever happen to them, but that through this tragedy, they had learned how comforting God could be. They said they never would have survived without God. They fully understood how strong their faith was, and what a rock the Word of God was in their life.

The rock-bottom fact of suffering is this: God is there for the believer in the midst of suffering. Jesus wept with Mary and Martha at the loss of their brother Lazarus, even knowing that He was about to raise Lazarus back to life. God weeps with you in your suffering.

There are a number of times in Scripture where God uses tragic circumstances or suffering to mold the character of a person. There are other instances in which He uses a tragedy as an opportunity to display His awesome miracle-working power. Jesus said this about the healing of a man who was born blind: "Neither this man nor his parents sinned, but that the works of God should be revealed in him." (John 9:3)

Quite frankly, I don't know how people get through life *without* God. Everyone at some point is going to suffer pain, rejection, loss in life, or some form of injury or disease. If you invite God into your life, He *will* be there for you in your time of suffering. He *will* be your rock and your fortress—your strength and your shelter in a time of trouble.

So, whether God is using our life's trials to discipline us, teach us, use us as an example for others, bring us closer to Himself, or strengthen us … we must take comfort that God is at work at all times for our *eternal* good. The Bible says, "We know that all things work together for good to those who love God." (Rom. 8:28)

Jesus said: "These things I have spoken to you, that in Me you may have peace. In the world you will have tribulation; but be of good cheer, I have overcome the world." (John 16:33)

The apostle Paul wrote: "And not only that, but we also glory in tribulations, knowing that tribulation produces perseverance; and perseverance, character; and character, hope. Now hope does not disappoint, because the love of God has been poured out in our hearts by the Holy Spirit who was given to us." (Rom. 5:3–5)

If anybody knew about suffering, it was the apostle Paul. There were those in the Corinthian church who were downgrading Paul as an apostle and Paul reminded the Corinthians,

> I am more: in labors more abundant, in stripes above measure, in prisons more frequently, in deaths often. From the Jews five times I received forty stripes minus one. Three times I was beaten with rods; once I was stoned; three times I was shipwrecked; a night and a day I have been in the deep; in journeys often, in perils of waters, in perils of robbers, in perils of my own countrymen, in perils of the Gentiles, in perils in the city, in perils in the wilderness, in perils in the sea, in perils among false brethren; in weariness and toil, in sleeplessness often, in hunger and thirst, in fastings often, in cold and nakedness—besides the other things, what comes upon me daily: my deep concern for all the churches. Who is weak, and I am not weak? Who is made to stumble, and I do not burn with indignation? If I must boast, I will boast in the things which concern my infirmity. (2 Cor. 11:23–30)

Paul went on to describe a "thorn in my flesh" which God would not remove. We don't know what this thorn was. It may have been recurring bouts of malaria or possibly blinding headaches. Whatever it was, this thorn in the flesh made it impossible for him to preach when he was suffering from its fierce attacks. This thorn also made him humble and an outstanding witness to others of how God can work even through our pain. Paul wrote, "He [the Lord] said to me, 'My grace is sufficient for you, for My strength is made perfect in weakness.' Therefore most gladly I will rather boast in my infirmities, that the power of Christ may rest upon me. Therefore I take pleasure in infirmities, in reproaches, in needs, in persecutions, in distresses, for Christ's sake. For when I am weak, then I am strong." (2 Cor. 12:9–10)

We are human. Human beings hurt. We get sick. We cry. We "feel." God knows. God cares. And God is *with* you, undergirding your humanity with His everlasting arms and His infinite love.

How should we respond to suffering?

James wrote: "Is anyone among you suffering? Let him pray. Is anyone cheerful? Let him sing psalms. Is anyone among you sick? Let him call for the elders of the church, and let them pray over him, anointing him with oil in the name of the Lord. And the prayer of faith will save the sick, and the Lord will raise him up. And if he has committed sins, he will be forgiven. Confess your trespasses to one another, and pray for one another, that you may be healed. The effective, fervent prayer of a righteous man avails much." (James 5:13–16)

THE BIBLE'S HELP
IN TIMES OF SORROW

One thing I know with great certainty. If you are suffering or are experiencing a hard time in your life, the Bible has a LOT to say to you. It can give you insights … guidance … and above all, hope. God never leaves His people without hope. He always holds out to us the hope of our salvation, the hope of eternal life with Him, the hope of our growing increasingly into the character likeness of Christ Jesus. There's an old Gospel song that says, "Because He lives, I can face tomorrow." How true!

Jesus doesn't promise us a life of wandering through a garden filled with rose bushes that don't have any thorns. What He does promise us is that He will never leave us or forsake us. He will walk through life's problems right by our side.

11

BENEFIT #5

THE SECRETS TO A SUCCESSFUL MARRIAGE AND FAMILY LIFE

O nce I started attending church regularly, I quickly realized that many people only go to church at Christmas and Easter ... and for weddings and funerals.

For them, the church is associated only with the happiest or saddest of times. The church has very little relevancy to their normal week-in, week-out lives.

GET ME TO THE CHURCH ON TIME

Almost every person I know dreams of having a "church wedding." And almost everyone wants a memorial service in a church when they die. I have always been amazed by the people who insist on a church service, but don't even have a church membership or know a pastor. I have been embarrassed for the deceased at funerals when the pastor in charge of the service acknowledges that he didn't even know the deceased, or he has to read comments about the deceased from note cards handed to him by family members. Let me ask you, If you died today, would your pastor know you well enough to say a few words about you at your memorial service without consulting any other person?

A good friend of mine, who is a pastor, once told me that he doesn't like doing weddings because nobody really pays attention to what he says. Everyone is more interested in how the bride, groom, and bridesmaids look. People are also waiting to see if someone wrote something nasty on the bottom of the groom's shoes when he bows at the altar rail for prayer! I'm not a prude. I believe weddings should be *fun* times of great celebration. But if a person doesn't fully intend to factor God into the marriage, why invite God to the wedding? Why not just have the ceremony in a beautiful building that has nothing to do with the Christian faith?

If two people are going to be married in a church, I hope they at least send God an invitation to the ceremony!

WHAT DOES THE BIBLE SAY ABOUT MARRIAGE?

In our nation, almost half of all marriages end in divorce. With that statistic in mind, it seems a good idea to me to see what the Bible has to say about marriage. There are entire books on what the Bible has to say about this subject and I certainly won't try to cover everything the Bible says in one short section of this book. Let me advise you this way: If you are anticipating marriage, or currently are struggling in your marriage, I recommend that you seek counseling from a church, *heed* that counseling, factor church attendance into your marriage, and inquire from your pastoral marriage counselor what books he or she recommends for you to read *as a couple*.

There are several aspects of marriage that clearly point to the relevancy of the Bible on this topic.

A Realistic, Serious Matter

I can't tell you how many young people I've met who are totally unrealistic about the concept of marriage. The fact is, marriage is not a fairy tale romance in which every moment is emotionally blissful. Especially if you marry young, you will live with your spouse longer than you will do anything else in your life. Your spouse will very likely be your foremost business partner, your child-raising partner, your social-entertaining partner, and ideally, your foremost prayer and Bible-reading partner.

At no time should marriage be entered into lightly. I have been married to my wife, Jan, for twenty-seven years at the time of this book's publication. I have a great wife! Since following and serving Christ has become the major focus of our life and home, our marriage has never been better. Even so, our marriage hasn't always been easy. I don't know of a good marriage that hasn't had its share of troubled moments.

A person needs to be prepared for bad times as well as good times in marriage. We've got to get beyond the idea in our society that if things aren't going well, divorce is the first option to consider.

Supportive, Not Corrective

Take time to get to know your partner well before marriage. It helps if the two people getting married have a lot in common. Neither the wife nor the husband should take on the role of a "marriage police officer." Marriage is not intended as a performance ground in which one spouse takes on the job of transforming or correcting the other, attempting to mold that spouse into his or her idea of perfection. It is also very important that if one spouse is a committed believer in Christ Jesus, the other spouse also be a believer.

Without a doubt, the Bible teaches that a spouse *may* be a key factor in bringing an unbelieving spouse to the Lord. However, the Bible also tells us that this is not always easy, and it isn't guaranteed. The Bible also tells us that in this, women very often set the example for bringing an unbelieving husband to the Lord: "Wives, likewise, be submissive to your own husbands, that even if some do not obey the word, they, without a word, may be won by the conduct of their wives, when they observe your chaste conduct accompanied by fear." (1 Pet. 3:1–2)

I can personally attest to the fact that in my marriage, it was my wife's actions that led me to the Lord. I was not a total "unbeliever in God" when we were married, but I was not actively seeking God and I certainly wasn't "close" to God. I had not accepted Jesus as my Savior. It was my wife who had the greatest influence on my decision to accept Jesus as my Savior, surrender my total life to Him, and seek to follow Him as my Lord.

I am also very willing to admit that my wife is the one most responsible for seeing that our children have become the fine young adults they are today. Both of them have accepted the Lord, are bright and talented, and are using their talents for Him. A schoolteacher for almost twenty years, Jan has been a great mom, teaching our children not only the basics of a good life, but also the essentials for a *godly* life.

Pray for Your Children's Future Spouses

A prayer that I believe all parents should pray for their children from the time of their birth, and increasingly as the years pass and they enter their teenage years, is that their children should date and marry Christians. A marriage between two people who are committed to doing things God's way holds out much greater potential for true happiness than a marriage between two people who are unsaved, or who are unequally yoked in their Christian faith.

SHOW ME A GOOD MARRIAGE AND I'LL SHOW YOU A GOOD WIFE

From my perspective, much of the work of a good marriage rests on a wife's shoulders. Women are the stronger and more reliable sex when it comes to matters of marriage and faith. That's not God speaking. That's me. If you show me a good marriage, I can nearly always find strong evidence that the marriage is good because the woman is a good *wife*. That certainly doesn't get husbands off the hook, however. The Bible says, "Husbands ought to love their own wives as their own bodies; he who loves his wife loves himself." (Eph. 5:28) It also says, "Husbands, likewise, dwell with them with understanding, giving honor to the wife, as to the weaker vessel, and as being heirs together of the grace of life, that your prayers may not be hindered." (1 Pet. 3:7)

God wants us to live in harmony with each other. He wants to be present in our homes. The Bible teaches, "Through wisdom a house is built, and by understanding it is established; by knowledge the rooms are filled with all precious and pleasant riches." (Prov. 24:3–4)

In our home, we have a plaque built into the wall near our front door. It quotes a simple Bible verse from the Book of Joshua: "But as for me and my house, we will serve the LORD." (Josh. 24:15)

If you are experiencing problems in your marriage, don't wait for them to escalate, compound, or grow! Seek godly counseling. I strongly encourage you to go to a *Christian* counselor who believes in the truth of God's Word.

FOUR VITAL PRACTICES WITHIN A FAMILY

Every good marriage —and every good parent-child relationship—shares these four common elements:

- Communication—frequent and meaningful
- Forgiveness—sincere, freely given and received
- Commitment—sincere and one hundred percent
- Kindness—nonstop and practical

A Full Commitment

I frequently hear people say that marriage is a 50-50 proposition. I disagree. It is a 100-100 proposition. Each spouse has to put the other spouse's interests first, one hundred percent of the time.

The same is true for being a parent. There are no 50-50 parent-child relationships. A parent has a hundred percent responsibility a hundred percent of the time.

A hundred percent commitment is hard. But if each spouse and each parent will have this level of commitment, a family can work and work well!

Sometimes it's hard ... but someone needs to be the first to say "I'm sorry." A person is only able to do this if their commitment to communication, forgiveness, commitment, and kindness is at a hundred-percent level.

Forgiveness Is a Sign of Strength

There are lots of different kinds of families, but one hallmark of quality family life is always this: Forgiveness. At the heart of all good relationships is a willingness to forgive. Jesus taught, "Forgive, and you will be forgiven." (Luke 6:37)

Forgiveness in the Bible is coupled with restitution. God told Moses that if any person sinned by deceiving or stealing from his neighbors, he should not only ask for forgiveness but he should be held responsible for righting the wrong. The Bible says, "He shall restore its full value, add one-fifth more to it, and give it to whomever it belongs." (Lev. 6:5) In another passage, God's Word says: "When a man or woman commits any sin that men commit in unfaithfulness against the Lord, and that person is guilty, then he shall confess the sin which he has done. He shall make restitution for his trespass in full value, plus one-fifth of it, and give it to the one he has wronged." (Num. 5:6–7)

THE BIBLE'S TEACHINGS ON MARRIAGE AND CHILDREN

The Bible has dozens and dozens of verses devoted to what it means to be a good spouse and a good parent. I'm going to let you do your homework and find those passages yourself. Below is a starting list of six passages on marriage and parenting:

- 1 Corinthians 7
- Ephesians 5:1–6:4
- Matthew 19:1–15
- 1 Peter 3:1–7
- Proverbs 31:10–31
- Colossians 3

I warn you in advance. You aren't always going to LIKE what you read in these passages, but I can also guarantee you this: What you read WORKS. It's God's plan. And if a person will line up their life with God's plan, and especially if two people will line up their lives together with God's plan, they CAN have a very successful marriage and family life.

Finally, I encourage you to read and reread … and then read again … the Book of Proverbs. There is a great deal of very practical wisdom in this book about being a parent and a spouse.

You'll also find a number of stories about godly spouses and parents in the Bible. I especially encourage you to read:

- The story of a woman named Abigail who not only survived a marriage to an abusive foolish man, but was rewarded for her excellence as a good wife. You can read about her in 1 Samuel 25.

- The story of a mother named Hannah who dedicated her son to God's service. Read about her in 1 Samuel 1 and 2:1–11.

- The story of two midwives named Shiphrah and Puah who refused to kill newborn babies even though Pharaoh had ordered them to do so. God rewarded them with children of their own. See Exodus 1.

- A wife who had the courage to speak the truth to her husband. See Esther 4–7.

- A mother who was willing to give her baby to another woman rather than see her child killed. See 1 Kings 3:16–28.

- A father who fasted and prayed for the healing of his son. See 2 Samuel 12:15–25.

- A father who, on his deathbed, charged his son to observe what the Lord requires, walk in His ways, and keep His commandments, so he might prosper in all he might attempt in his life. See 1 Kings 2:2–3.

The Bible also has a number of stories about *bad* spouses and parents, and the terrible consequences that resulted from their actions … but I'll leave you to discover those stories on your own!

12

BENEFIT #6

KNOWING WHAT YOU REALLY BELIEVE WITH CONFIDENCE

I mentioned in a previous chapter that I took a quantum leap in my Christian life when I moved from "believing in God" to "believing God." Let me tell you how that happened.

The year 1992 was the year I began spending more time with the Bible. I had joined Second Baptist Church of Houston. The pastor, Dr. Ed Young, is one of the most dynamic speakers I have ever heard. He truly is one of the world's greatest pastors. There is a difference between the two. There are many good speakers who don't know the Word of God. There are also wonderfully devoted pastors and priests who are not very good speakers. It is a powerful combination when someone is both a great speaker and a great pastor.

I believe that if Dr. Young hadn't chosen the teaching of God's Word as his life's work, he would have been among the world's top motivational speakers. It's no mystery to me that his nationally broadcast show, *The Winning Walk,* is a success. I know the man behind the camera. What he says is genuine because of who he is.

Dr. Young was a guest on my radio show one day. Even though my show usually covers topical events and political issues, I also like to discuss spiritual issues. I try to bring a Biblical perspective to current events and the audience seems to like the fact that I do. I now do a show once a month called *The God Squad.* I have a panel of three guests: an evangelical pastor, a Catholic priest, and a Jewish rabbi to talk about Biblical issues and take questions from the audience.

The station I operate is not a "Christian" radio station, per se. But there is no question that we have developed a format where the Word of God is a major part of our programming.

Dr. Young knew I had a heart for the Lord, but from our conversation, he also knew I needed a church home. A few hours after he left the studio I got a call from one of his associate pastors, Craig Reynolds. Craig, a former shortstop for the Mariners and Astros, was one of the professional athletes I had noticed years earlier in my sportscasting days as being in that small group of athletes who served God and had their career in proper perspective.

Craig was a person whom God has used to plant lots of good seeds in the garden of my life through the years. We had a number of good conversations about his relationship with the Lord. I admired him as a father and husband, as well as a shortstop who made the All-Star team. It had been almost ten years since we had spoken, but I was glad to accept his invitation to lunch.

When we met over lunch he told me that after baseball he had gone on to a very successful career as a stockbroker. But then, even though his new career was financially rewarding, he sought a job that gave him greater meaning. He had become a pastor. He invited me to join Second Baptist and I did.

The more I attended church, the more interested I became in learning more about God's plan for my life.

My wife remains Catholic. I jokingly say that we have a "mixed marriage"—Baptist and Catholic—and that our children, who attend both churches and have been confirmed in the Catholic church, are really "Baptlic." I also joke that my son, who graduated from Baylor University, a Baptist school in Texas, finished with a minor in evangelical bingo calling.

Our so-called mixed marriage has never been a problem. Jan attends my church and I attend hers. I am close friends with her priest and she with Dr. Young. There *are* differences between the Catholic and Protestant faiths, but the important thing is that we both love the Lord and believe in Jesus Christ as the Son of God for our salvation.

During my time of renewed study and interest in THE MOST IMPORTANT BOOK YOU'LL EVER READ, the HOLY BIBLE, I experienced a great surge in my faith. I came to embrace the Bible's teachings more and more. I found that I didn't want to go through a day without reading something from God's Word.

Then it suddenly occurred to me that I needed to move from "believing in God" to "believing God."

There is a world of difference between those two thought processes. Except for a very small percentage of people in the world who call themselves atheists, almost everyone believes in some type of God (or the potential for some kind of God to exist). Even the devil and his followers believe in the existence of God.

Believing God, however, is different than believing God exists. Believing God means that you accept what God has to say in His

Word as being directly for your life. Believing God goes beyond believing in the authenticity of the Bible—it is *accepting* what the Bible says as being true for *you*.

God isn't a practical joker. He didn't inspire the Bible to be written over several centuries—all of the principles and concepts of the Bible hinging together into a wonderful whole—only to say, "I didn't mean it." In the New Testament, the apostle Paul wrote to his ministry co-worker Timothy, "All Scripture is given by inspiration of God, and is profitable for doctrine, for reproof, for correction, for instruction in righteousness, that the man of God may be complete, thoroughly equipped for every good work." (2 Tim. 3:16–17)

I either had to accept the Bible and its teachings in its entirety, or throw it all away. It became an all-or-nothing issue to me. The Bible is not some type of spiritual salad bar in which a person gets to pick and choose what he"likes." None of us has the privilege of choosing those parts of the Bible that make us feel comfortable and discarding the rest. What arrogance and pride that is—to think *we* are wise enough to decide which parts of God's Word are true and which might not be!

Choosing to *believe God* was a quantum leap in my faith walk.

As I stated earlier, some people don't read the Bible out of sheer apathy. Others don't read it because it means an end to their guilt-free living. I fell into that second category. I didn't *want* to know what God had to say about my life. I intuitively knew that if I was going to live the way God wanted me to live, I'd have to change some things that I didn't want to change. The only alternative, of course, was to continue living with guilt.

Changing isn't nearly as difficult as living with an abiding sense of guilt. I chose to change.

CHANGE...
FOR THE
SAKE OF GROWTH

God doesn't ask us to change just for the sake of change. Neither does He ask us to change things in our lives just so He can strip away all the things that we consider to be fun or "self-directed." God requires that we change so that we might truly become all that He created us to be.

I really had no option but to "believe God."

There were still many things I didn't understand about the Bible. I still have questions about specific passages today. There never will be a time when I, or anyone else for that matter, will "understand all the Bible." But I can say this, I understand more today than I understood a decade ago!

Every time we read a certain book or verse in the Bible, no matter how many times we may have read it before, God reveals more of its meaning to us.

There are many verses I understand now that I didn't understand the first time I read them. As far as the parts I don't fully understand, I can still accept the truth of those verses by choosing to *believe* God … in other words, I accept them by faith. The Bible says, "Trust in the LORD with all your heart, and lean not on your own understanding; in all your ways acknowledge Him, and He shall direct your paths." (Prov. 3:5–6)

When you begin to *believe* God, and in turn, *believe* what the Bible says is true for *you*, every thing in your life is suddenly subject to reexamination. That certainly was my experience!

THE KEY QUESTION REGARDING "BELIEVING"

The Bible tells us the key statement that is related to all believing. It is a statement made by an angel who was visiting a young virgin girl in Nazareth. He said, "With God nothing will be impossible." (Luke 1:37)

That single concept—NOTHING is impossible with God—is the foundation for all of our believing.

Can God change a human heart?

Can God forgive a vile sinner?

Can God heal a sick body?

Can God move mountains to accomplish His purposes?

The answer of faith is a resounding "YES!" Why? Because … nothing is impossible with God.

God can do all things because God is above all things, the creator of all things, and more powerful than all other sources of power. He has unlimited resources, infinite wisdom, and a depth of love and purpose that are beyond human calculation.

How can a man stay alive in a great fish for three days and not die? I don't know. But … nothing is impossible with God. Especially since the Bible tells us that God "prepared" that great fish. (See Jonah 1:17.) And by the way, the Bible never says the fish was a whale.

How can three men who are tossed into a vastly overheated furnace come out alive? I don't know. But … nothing is impossible with God. (You can read all about this in Daniel 3.)

How can a person survive a night in a den of hungry lions? How can a man walk on water? How can water come out of a rock? How can an ax head float? I don't know! But … nothing is impossible with God. (You can read about these incidents in the

Bible in Daniel 6, Matthew 14:22–36, Exodus 17:1–7, and 2 Kings 6:1–5.)

Two of the major miracles of the Bible are ones that seem to be a stumbling block to believing for a number of people: the virgin birth of Jesus and the resurrection of Jesus. Let's take a look at these miracles.

WHAT ABOUT THE VIRGIN BIRTH?

The birth of Jesus was prophesied in the Old Testament about eight hundred years before His birth. The great prophet Isaiah said, "Therefore the Lord Himself will give you a sign: Behold, the virgin shall conceive and bear a Son, and shall call His name Immanuel." (Is. 7:14) Immanuel is a descriptive name for Jesus.

Matthew confirms this prophecy in the New Testament, writing about how the Lord appeared in a dream to Joseph, the husband of Mary, saying, "She will bring forth a Son, and you shall call His name JESUS, for He will save His people from their sins." The Bible says, "All this was done that it might be fulfilled which was spoken by the Lord through the prophet, saying, 'Behold, a virgin shall be with child, and bear a Son, and they shall call His name Immanuel,' which is translated, 'God with us.'" (See Matt. 1:21–22.)

I find it interesting today that people readily believe in "cloning" but they cannot believe in the virgin birth. The biology is very similar! In cloning, a single cell of an adult animal is caused to divide in such a way that the genetic material in the cell replicates an entire physical organism. Is it so impossible that God the Holy Spirit could cause, through His all-powerful divine means, a single cell in an unmarried virgin named Mary to divide so that the genetic material in an egg in her womb could become the basis for the creation of an entire physical organism?

At the heart of doubt about the virgin birth is the question, "Is anything too difficult for God?" Mary, herself, questioned how she might become pregnant and give birth to a son since she was a virgin.

The angel Gabriel who came to her with the pronouncement that she had been chosen to bear Jesus, said to her, "The Holy Spirit will come upon you, and the power of the Highest will overshadow you; therefore, also, that Holy One who is to be born will be called the Son of God." The angel then told her that Elizabeth, her relative, was going to bear a child in her old age—even though she was past childbearing years and had been barren all her life to that point. The angel concluded, "With God nothing will be impossible." (See Luke 1:30–37.)

Mary believed that *nothing* was impossible with God. She responded to the angel, "Behold the maidservant of the Lord! Let it be to me according to your word." (Luke 1:38)

When it comes right down to it…

God drawing His people out of Egypt via a dry-land path through a sea…is no greater or lesser miracle than the birth of Jesus.

Jesus feeding five thousand families by dividing a few bits of fish and bread … is no greater or lesser miracle than the birth of Jesus.

The Holy Spirit transforming a human heart and giving us a "spiritual rebirth"… is no greater or lesser miracle than the birth of Jesus.

All of these miracles are impossible in the natural. But … NOTHING is impossible with God.

WHAT ABOUT THE RESURRECTION?

The resurrection of Jesus is a point of doubt for some people. The Bible states that after Jesus died on the cross, His body was wrapped in burial cloths, along with about seventy-five pounds of spices, and it was laid in a previously unused tomb owned by a man named Joseph of Arimathea. Jewish officials, fearing that the apostles might come and steal the body and claim Jesus was still alive, asked Pilate the Roman governor to post a guard at the tomb, including an official seal placed on the stone that covered the tomb. Pilate agreed to this.

On the first day of the week (the Sunday after the Friday on which Jesus was crucified), several women followers of Jesus went to the tomb to renew the spices. They found the stone covering the tomb had been rolled away, and inside, they found the tomb empty—except for the linen cloth that had been placed over Jesus' face, and the long strips of cloth and spices that had been wrapped around His body. The long strips of cloth and spices were in a heap on the stone slab where His body had been laid, unwrapped—as if the body had simply disappeared from within them. The linen face cloth was neatly folded up and placed in the corner of the tomb.

Two angels appeared to the women and said to them, "Why do you look for the living among the dead? He is not here; He has risen! Remember how He told you, while He was still with you in Galilee: 'The Son of Man must be delivered into the hands of sinful men, be crucified and on the third day be raised again.'" The women remembered…and went rushing back to the eleven disciples with this news (the disciple Judas who had betrayed Jesus had already committed suicide at this point). (See Luke 24:5–8.)

What happened to the body?

If the Romans or Jewish leaders had taken the body, surely they would have taken it wrapped as it was—and then put it on display as evidence that Jesus was truly dead. Even if they had unwrapped the body later, surely they wouldn't have left the strips of cloth in a body-shaped heap on the burial slab, or have removed the face cloth and neatly folded it to one side.

If Christian followers of Jesus had taken the body, they would have had to overcome an official guard (a group of four stalwart Roman soldiers), roll away a stone that had been officially sealed by the Roman guards (likely tied and staked with ropes), unwrapped the body and then rewrapped the burial cloths and spices to make it appear that the cloths had been undisturbed, and then escaped through the garden and streets of Jerusalem carrying a naked corpse without anybody spotting them.

And then, what were the apostles to do with the body? They would have to rewrap and rebury it … and where might all this be done in such great secrecy that *none* of them or any of their relatives would ever betray the secret? Jerusalem was overrun by thousands of people at the time of the Passover Feast! And *then*, they would have to agree secretly to live and DIE, even under intense persecution and horrible death sentences, without ever changing, altering, justifying, or revealing their secret. Talk about implausible!

Or, Jesus rose from the dead just as He had said. Once again, God had done the miraculous and the seemingly impossible.

By the way, the folded face cloth was a sign that people at that time recognized. When a guest was served a banquet feast, he usually was given a cloth to use in wiping his hands. If the guest was pleased with the feast and hoped to return again to the host's table, he would crumple the cloth and leave it at his plate, signifying by this symbolic act that he hoped to return soon to pick up his cloth and resume eating. If the guest, however, had no intent of ever returning again to that particular banquet site, he would neatly fold his cloth and leave it, signifying that he never again intended to return to that table to eat of that fare. Jesus was sending a very direct Jewish signal that He had died once and for all, and that He would never again return to a tomb!

THE PURPOSE OF THE MIRACLES

God's miracles throughout the Bible were not intended to "wow" either the unbelievers or the faithful. They had a *purpose*—to show God's unlimited power to provide, protect, and preserve His people. They showed God's power over all manner of sickness, disease, calamity, natural occurrence, and death itself.

The miracles were not intended to "confuse" people or to generate doubt. They were intended to bolster *faith*.

Just as some people misinterpret or don't understand the miracles of the Bible, some people question why Jesus spoke at times in what seemed to be a "veiled" way so that the truth wasn't readily obvious.

In the case of the parables, Jesus used this form of communication to CALL people to have faith, because it was only on the other side of believing that some of the things He taught could be fully understood.

Parables are stories that make a spiritual point. On one occasion the disciples of Jesus asked Him why He taught using stories. He replied, "Because it has been given to you to know the mysteries of the kingdom of heaven, but to them it has not been given. For whoever has [faith in Me], to him more will be given, and he will have abundance; but whoever does not have, even what he has will be taken away from him. Therefore I speak to them in parables, because seeing they do not see, and hearing they do not hear, nor do they understand." (Matt. 13:11–13)

This passage may *sound* as if Jesus was trying to veil the truth and keep secrets. Not at all. The "them" in the above passage referred to religious leaders who were striving to keep the *letter* of the law, including more than a thousand manmade laws that weren't in the Bible, but who were not keeping the "spirit" of the law or responding in *faith*. What Jesus was saying is that it takes *faith* to understand the spiritual truth of parables. Believing comes first—which is the act of using one's faith—and understanding follows. There are certain principles of Jesus' teaching that simply cannot be understood until after a person chooses to *believe*. Those who choose to believe have "eyes to see" and "ears to hear." Those who don't choose to believe find that even what they *think* they know with certainty about the letter of the law is likely to be called into question or doubted over time.

Jesus never tried to hide the truth from those who sincerely wanted to know it. He did not, however, wish to give ammunition to those religious leaders who were out to persecute Him.

A CONFIRMATION OF THE TRUTH

I am certain of one thing when it comes to believing and knowing with certainty what I believe. It's this: God ALWAYS confirms His word to us. The same is true for the message of the Bible. The Bible says that it is out of the mouth of TWO witnesses that the truth is established. God will accompany the truth of His written Word, the Bible, with the truth of His ongoing spoken word to your heart. He will reveal to you as you apply the Bible that the Bible is *true* in your life. The truth of the Bible is established in us as we see it work in our own lives.

That happened to me in a dramatic way on a trip to the least likely of places, "sin city," Las Vegas, Nevada.

VIVA LAS VEGAS

In 1992, two years after we had purchased the second radio station, I was asked to go to Las Vegas to a national television and radio convention. The Chairman of the Board of a company that owned a number of radio stations wanted to talk to me about buying our two stations. My partners weren't particularly interested in selling, but they thought I should go and at least listen to their offer.

The meeting was scheduled for about thirty minutes but it lasted nearly two hours. I left the room with an offer that meant my partners and I could retire our debt, have a financial cushion for life, and we would still have our jobs as managers of the stations. The offer was one that meant I would no longer be under intense financial pressure.

I went back to my hotel exhilarated and in awe at what God seemed to be doing. Only seven years earlier, I had been financially defeated—"flat broke" as we say in Texas. I knew my limitations—I wasn't smart enough to have orchestrated the last seven years. I wasn't that talented, I wasn't a visionary. I instinctively knew that this was all a "God thing."

Time and again, out of nowhere it seemed, jobs and people and money had appeared. The tough, dark years of financial ruin in the restaurant business suddenly made more sense. The Bible says, "We also glory in tribulations, knowing that tribulation produces perseverance; and perseverance, character; and character, hope. Now hope does not disappoint, because the love of God has been poured out in our hearts by the Holy Spirit who was given to us." (Rom. 5:3–5)

I had an awesome sense that God had been preparing me for the opportunity He had for me all along. He had been forging perseverance and character and hope in me. If I had not gone through certain failures, I would have not been prepared for certain successes. I would not have learned important lessons about managing people.

I knew one thing with great certainty: God was at work. The deal was *His*.

I immediately called for a cab and had the driver take me to a church I had seen near the Tropicana Hotel, the Shrine of the Most Holy Redeemer. It was the middle of the day and I feel sure the cabbie thought I was going there to pray before making a big bet, or going to ask forgiveness because I had lost a lot of money. I have been back to that church several times over the years and the doors have *always* been locked during the middle of the day. But on that particular day I first went there, the door was open.

I went inside. No one was there.

Have you ever been in a large church all by yourself? The feeling was both strange and wonderful to me. I felt very close to God, as if He and I were alone together in that space. Although I had been baptized fourteen years earlier, I got down on my knees and prayed as I have never prayed before or since.

I asked God's forgiveness for all of my sins. I repented of my sinful life and choosing to pursue in so many cases "Dan's Plan." I asked God to forgive me for factoring Him out of my life for much of the last fifteen years. I thanked God for not factoring me out of His plans. I cried like a child. And I asked for one more opportunity to move forward in my life, fully dedicating my business, my talents, and all that I had to Him.

In that hour, I not only asked Him to come into my life as my Savior, but to be my *Master and Lord.*

When I got up off my knees and walked back to the hotel, I never felt better in my life. From that moment on, I have had a great boldness about sharing the Word...a deep inner peace about the future ... a calm about the day-to-day problems of life...and an inner smile that just won't end. It is an awesome feeling to know that you will live forever. It is an equally awesome feeling to know that God is your Lord—guiding you and leading you every step of the way until you enter eternity. That is what the Bible promises to all believers. I finally decided that day to take God up on His promise.

I felt like a new person after that encounter with God in the Shrine of the Most Holy Redeemer. Family members, friends, and business associates also saw a difference in my life. In fact, the listeners of my radio show repeatedly told me that they were hearing a bolder, more outspoken man for Christ. They also noticed a man more at peace and more confident about life.

After that trip to Las Vegas, I was convinced more than ever that God wanted to use our radio station as an outlet for His Word in the fourth largest city in our nation. Our station reached almost 400,000 listeners a week. It made us the largest potential "outsource" for ministry in Houston.

I did not lose sight of the fact that unlike many churches, what we say on the air is not "preaching to the choir." At the time, we were a secular station with shows such as those syndicated by Rush Limbaugh and Dr. Laura Schlessinger. I believed we truly had a chance to make a difference in people's lives by the shows we aired. We had a chance to reach out to those who were hurting, searching, and who seldom, if ever, had heard the Word of God.

I am continually amazed at how many people have never heard Biblical principles explained, or have never been told how to apply Biblical concepts to their lives. I know in my heart that there are thousands of people within the sound of my voice every day now who are just waiting to hear the Gospel. Many of them are EAGER to believe, they just don't know what to believe. Others are EAGER to hear confirm with certainty what they *think* they believe.

What about you today?

Have you settled in your mind and heart what you believe *with certainty* about Jesus? Have you settled in your heart and mind that you are not only going to believe in Him as your Savior, but also follow Him as your Lord? Have you really settled with certainty in your soul that NOTHING is impossible with God?

13

BENEFIT #7

LEARNING WHAT GOD HAS TO SAY ABOUT MONEY

Let me make something very clear as we begin this chapter. I am not writing this book to get rich. God has already met my needs. The profits from this book will go directly back into printing and marketing more books so that more people might be inspired to read their Bibles. This is God's project. I just feel honored that He chose me to have a part.

Many people I know put up barriers in their heart and mind almost instantly when they hear the words God and money used in the same sentence. They hold to an opinion that "all the church wants is my money" or that "the preacher only cares about how much I give." The fact is that the Bible has a great deal to say about money. Jesus taught more about money than He did heaven or hell! And why is that? I believe it is because we live in a very practical, material world. We need money to survive. We need to know how to manage our money and other resources wisely. And most of all, we need to come to grips with our attitudes about money. The state of our spiritual life is directly related in many ways to how we manage money and material possessions.

I have also discovered that many people have great misconceptions about what the Bible actually *says* about financial matters. So let me give you a very quick short course on money.

Basic Bible Principles About Giving and Getting

One of the most basic Biblical principles related to giving is this: don't look for reward or honor from your giving. (See Matt. 6:2–4.) That is one of the most common conceptions about giving in the world at large. People just don't give, normally, unless their name goes on the building or they are listed in the "arts" program in bold lettering.

The Bible teaches that the size of the gift isn't what matters, but rather, that we give according to what we have been given. The Bible teaches: "Where your treasure is, there your heart will be also." (Matt. 6:21)

The Bible plan for giving is the tithe, or ten percent. I remember asking one time if that ten percent was to come off gross income or take-home (net) pay. I got a quick response, "Do you want God to bless you in gross or net blessings?"

If we are going to do what the Bible says, and we are believing God and not just believing in God, then we are going to *want* to tithe according to His plan, not ours.

I recently heard about a very successful church in New York City that has a very long tradition. It is part of a mainline denomination. A decade ago, however, the church was about to close its doors. Its membership was small, elderly, and therefore, dying and growing smaller by the month. A new pastor came to the church and made radical changes, including an abundance of sermons on giving. He gave as his reason that Jesus taught more about material giving and financial matters than about any other singular topic. Why? From this pastor's perspective, Jesus did this because He knew that a giving spirit was the key to receiving personal blessings, and that a giving spirit within any community was going to raise both the spiritual and material water tables of everybody involved. God's plan for giving *works*—and it works at many levels.

Giving in the Bible goes all the way back to the time of Abraham. The Bible tells us "Abraham gave a tenth part of all." (Heb. 7:2) The Law of Moses taught that a person should give a tenth of everything as a tithe: "You shall truly tithe all the increase of your grain that the field produces year by year." (Deut. 14:22) (The word "tithe" means "tenth.")

The Bible doesn't limit giving to the tithe, of course. It teaches that if you can give more, do so.

There's one key aspect to giving a "tenth" that even many believers seem to overlook. I missed it at first. The tenth is to be taken out of our *firstfruits* of labor. The Bible says, "Honor the Lord with your possessions, and with the firstfruits of all your increase, so your barns will be filled with plenty, and your vats will overflow with new wine." (Prov. 3:9–10)

The tithe comes off the top…it's not a matter of what may be "left over" at the end of the month.

GIVING OFF THE TOP MEANS PAYING GOD FIRST

What people do with their money *first* is usually what is most important to them. The financial advisors of today have a common phrase: "Pay yourself first." They are referring to putting money aside into savings or long-term investments. The Bible says we are to pay God first.

Both Faithful and Joyful

God expects us to be both *faithful* and *joyful* in our giving. The Bible teaches that "God loves a cheerful giver." (2 Cor. 9:7) A person who believes that he is being *forced* to make gifts, financial or otherwise, is rarely a cheerful giver. Be enthusiastic about what you give. Feel good about where you give and to what you give. Find something that motivates you to the point where you can hardly wait to give because you want to see what God will do with your gift to move His Kingdom forward and bless your life!

Wise in Our Choices

"But *everybody* seems to be asking for money," you may say. True. Once people find out that you are generous with your time, talents, and money, you likely will be asked by many people to give to many different causes. Very few people are wealthy enough to give time or money to *every* cause—in fact, I don't know of any person who is wealthy enough to give to *every* person who requests money.

I learned an important principle from one of my close friends and business partners, Mike Richards. When he is approached about making a gift, he tells the person that he will give him permission to ask, if he will be given permission to say "yes" or "no." Mike also lets the person know he only gives to concerns that are willing to "match" in some way what he gives. This gives the asker added incentive, and also assures my partner that whatever his level of giving, it's going to be doubled in effectiveness for the charitable cause.

My partner chooses his charities very carefully. He has a special heart for certain causes and he focuses his giving in those areas. He also taught me the value of his choosing upfront—as in the first few days of January—the places where he intends to plant his giving during the year. If others ask after that point, he simply tells them that he has already committed his giving for the year but if they want to send him information for consideration the following year, he'll read it and pray about it.

Giving should be a wonderful experience for you. Don't let anyone make you feel badly about it. If you are doing what God has commanded, then God will be pleased.

THE CORE TRUTH ABOUT MONEY: GOD OWNS IT ALL

Many times I hear Christians and others say, "I'm giving God His part." They are referring to the tenth. The fact is, God owns *everything*. The Bible says, "He is called the God of the whole earth." (Is. 54:5) The Psalmist said, "God *is* the King of all the earth." (Ps. 47:7)

God lays claim to *all* of us at the time we accept Jesus as our Savior. He *owns* His creation—this earth and all its resources. He *allows* wealth to come into our hands. When we give back to God, we aren't giving Him "God's part." We are giving to the Lord "a portion of what is already His!" This change in perspective greatly changed my giving. I used to ask myself, "How much of my money should I give to God?" Now I ask, "How much of God's money should I keep for myself?"

For me personally, I have found it very beneficial to match the dollars I spend on certain personal items with dollars to particular ministry causes. For example, if I spend a significant amount of money on a luxury item or a trip for my family or myself, which I personally define as anything that runs a thousand dollars or more, I try to give that same amount away in *extra* giving beyond the tithe. Not everyone can do that ... but many people can.

Paying "Back Tithes"

Let me challenge you with an extreme idea. Not everyone can do this, or will want to do this. I'm not even suggesting you do this. But I'm challenging you to think about the idea. It has meant a great deal to me.

Since I didn't become a committed Christian until later in life, I had not given a tithe of my earnings for many years. I sat down and calculated all the money I had earned during those years when I wasn't following Christ and calculated what my tithe *should* have been. Most people I know can remember fairly accurately what they have made each year—they know when they received raises or had bad years. Most of us have our tax returns for many years. It turned into a fun exercise for me.

Then, I calculated what ten percent should have been and I made a decision that I would begin to give "extra" to the Lord's work until I had paid that amount. Certainly God doesn't expect us to "even up the books" when we become a Christian. It was just something I wanted to do.

Give to the Right Causes

Be sure your gifts aren't wasted. Don't be reluctant to ask questions about how your money is going to be spent. There are many needy ministries and charities that truly need help and will spend your money wisely.

Time and time again, I have seen God keep His promise of entrusting people who give with *more*. In the vast majority of cases, those who are good stewards of their God-given resources are given *significantly* more over which to be good stewards! I have also seen, time and time again, people whose goal in life was to store up more for themselves than for God. They have found that their hoarded money brought them pain and misery. Many times, they simply lost what they should have given in the first place. Sometimes they lost all they had.

While a few of the Wall Street tycoons and business barons of a hundred years ago gave generously to philanthropic causes, there were many more who died broken men. The Bible says plainly:

> Command those who are rich in this present age not to be haughty, nor to trust in uncertain riches but in the living God, who gives us richly all things to enjoy. Let them do good, that they be rich in good works, ready to give, willing to share, storing up for themselves a good foundation for the time to come, that they may lay hold on eternal life. (1 Tim. 6:17–19)

A GIVING SPIRIT AND A GREEDY SPIRIT CAN'T COEXIST

Part of God's plan for our prosperity is that we be generous and faithful givers to His work. The Bible says about our giving: "Give, and it will be given to you: good measure, pressed down, shaken together, and running over will be put into your bosom. For with the same measure that you use, it will be measured back to you." (Luke 6:38)

The Bible also says, "He who sows sparingly will also reap sparingly, and he who sows bountifully will also reap bountifully." (2 Cor. 9:6)

The better we function as stewards, the more God entrusts to us. What God cannot tolerate is greed. To be greedy is to disobey God's commands to give and to give generously ... it is to fail to trust God to meet all of our needs even as we give generously ... and it is to cause harm—even eternal harm—to another person, somewhere, even a person we may have never met. To greedily hoard for ourselves something that rightfully should be given to the extension of the Gospel and the care-taking of the needy is a sin. Jesus taught a parable about this as well:

> The ground of a certain rich man yielded plentifully. And he thought within himself, saying, "What shall I do, since I have no room to store my crops?" So he said, "I will do this: I will pull down my barns and build greater, and there I will store all my crops and my goods. And I will say to my soul, 'Soul, you have many goods laid up for many years; take your ease; eat, drink, and be merry.'" But God said to him, "You fool! This night your soul will be required of you; then whose will those things be which you have provided?"
>
> So is he who lays up treasure for himself, and is not rich toward God. (Luke 12:16–21)

God doesn't have anything against people having nice homes or material possessions. He is against our trusting in those possessions ... our taking pride in our possessions...and in our storing up things for ourselves *without being generous toward the work of the Lord.* Throughout God's Word you will find many commands to care for those who are sick, needy, friendless, and oppressed—the strangers, the widows, and the orphans. You will find many commands to give the tithe to God's work.

Those who fail to give reap the consequences of their disobedience and greedy pride.

Those who give generously also reap a tremendous reward.

Read what God's Word says according to the prophet Malachi:

"Return to Me, and I will return to you," says the LORD of hosts.

"But you said, 'In what way shall we return?'

"Will a man rob God? Yet you have robbed Me!

"But you say, 'In what way have we robbed You?'

"In tithes and offerings. You are cursed with a curse, for you have robbed Me, even this whole nation. Bring all the tithes into the storehouse that there may be food in My house, and try Me now in this," says the LORD of hosts, "If I will not open for you the windows of heaven and pour out for you such blessing that there will not be room enough to receive it.

"And I will rebuke the devourer for your sakes, so that he will not destroy the fruit of your ground, nor shall the vine fail to bear fruit for you in the field," says the LORD of hosts; "And all nations will call you blessed, for you will be a delightful land." (Mal. 3:7–12)

WARNING AGAINST THE LOVE OF MONEY

So many people take verses about money out of their context in the Bible, or they misquote what the Bible says about money. Many people misquote the Bible in saying, "Money is the root of all evil." The Bible actually says, "For the love of money is a root of all kinds of evil, for which some have strayed from the faith in their greediness, and pierced themselves through with many sorrows." (1 Tim. 6:10) The foremost sin about money is a *love of money*.

It is not a sin to have wealth. It is a sin to love money and to trust in your own ability to get wealth, to fail to see wealth as coming from the Lord, and to fail in honoring God with your generous giving as you receive money, earnings, and possessions.

I once heard Bill O'Reilly say on his national radio program that greed is behind all the problems in the world. I agree. People are greedy for wealth and power. Greed wrecks marriages, friendships, families, and businesses.

Jesus gave a wonderful illustration about people who trust in their money. He said, "It is easier for a camel to go through the eye of a needle than for a rich man to enter the kingdom of God." (Matt. 19:24)

Does this mean that nobody with money goes to heaven? Does this mean that if you have more than what is required to meet your bare necessities you must give it all away? No. We need to read what Jesus said in the light of what an "eye of the needle" was in Jesus' time.

City gates in Jesus' day were large, often double-door gates. When open, horse-drawn carts and camels laden with the goods of caravans could easily pass through them. At night, these large gates were officially closed and barred. Only a door-sized opening cut into the side of one of the large gates gave access to people who might have been outside the city when the gates were closed. These smaller doorways set into a larger gate were called an "eye of the needle."

Now, a camel *could* get through such a small door after hours, but only with great effort. All of the goods on its back would need to be set aside, and then the camel would need to get down on its knees and scoot itself along the dirt in something of a crawling fashion. It wasn't an easy job to convince a camel to do that!

Jesus was pointing out that the rich are very often reluctant to give up anything they are "carrying" through life, especially if it requires the humility of bowing before God.

The disciples spoke privately with Jesus after He had given this illustration. The Bible says, "When His disciples heard it, they were exceedingly amazed, saying, 'Who then can be saved?' But Jesus looked at them and said to them, 'With men this is impossible, but with God all things are possible.'" (Matt. 19:25–26) It is against human nature to want to give up anything of our excess to God's work. It takes a heart-changing, life-transforming miracle of God for a person to *desire* to give away his wealth.

At issue is the heart of a man or woman, not the savings account of a person. If a person is faithfully tithing and giving offerings, and is willing to give up anything that he has at the time the Lord requests it, he is in no danger of the Lord's chastisement.

Jesus taught, "For where your treasure is, there your heart will be also." (Matt. 6:21)

Let's face it. Money *is* important to each one of us. People need to eat, wear clothes, have shelter, educate their children, have transportation to get to and from work, and so forth. I've been broke and I've had sufficient money. It's far easier to have sufficient money!

We also must face the Word of God. He commands us to give a tithe to the storehouse of the Lord—in plain language, that's ten percent to the church. That's the bare minimum requirement for obedience to God. The Lord then puts His added blessing on our giving of offerings that are beyond the ten percent. He requires this giving for two main reasons. First, so the financial needs of the church can be met and the outreach work of the church can move forward. And second, so people in need can receive help. Those in spiritual need must have spiritual help—they need to hear the good news about Jesus as their Savior. Those in material or physical need must have material or physical help.

God doesn't just require the giving of our money, of course. He also requires the giving of our time and talents. There are countless ways one can help another person in need without the giving of money. America's number-one export is volunteerism. We are a generous nation with our money and our time…and may it ever be so. One person's talents and time may be just as valuable as another person's money.

God never places importance on the size of a financial gift, but rather, He requires the giving of a percentage. A person who makes $15,000 a year and gives $1,500 to the Lord's house is just as much in right standing before God as a person who makes $150,000 a year and gives $15,000 to the church. In fact, the former person is probably making a bigger sacrifice.

God's plan is totally equitable. His plan works!

Let me ask you today: How willing are you to give of what you have to extend God's purposes on this earth? The Bible says, "For if there is first a willing mind, it is accepted according to what one has, and not according to what he does not have." (2 Cor. 8:12)

GIVING CAN BE A VERY HUMBLING EXPERIENCE

One of the great lessons that I've learned through giving is that giving can be a very humbling experience. Let me give you an illustration of this. I don't say what I'm about to say to win your applause or approval, but rather, to tell you about those who GIVE far more than money.

I give money regularly to the International Bible Society (IBS). This organization is the largest translator of Bibles in the world. Their goal is to get a Bible, or a portion of the Bible, into enough languages so that every person in the world has an opportunity to read the Word of God for himself or herself.

We're spoiled in the United States. Any person can go to a wide variety of stores and purchase a Bible. We have them provided to us free in hotel and motel rooms! In many nations of the world, Bibles are extremely difficult to find and even more costly to own. In some nations, a person is likely to be imprisoned or killed for owning or distributing Bibles.

There are approximately 6,600 different dialects and languages worldwide. As of 2002, the complete Bible has only been translated into approximately 250 of them. The good news is that these translations are understood by almost half of the world's population, but there is still a lot of work to be done.

The Bible says that before Jesus returns, all the world will have had an opportunity to hear the Gospel. Jesus said, "The gospel must first be preached to all the nations." (Mark 13:10) This does not mean that every person in the world will accept the Gospel, but all will be given an opportunity to hear and accept.

The ability to translate the Scriptures has been greatly enhanced by the development of computers. The work is proceeding more rapidly than ever. And with the advent of the World Wide Web, the day is drawing closer when everyone truly *will* have the Word of God available in a language he or she can understand.

Each year I have the opportunity to meet some of the people who are risking their lives to print and distribute Bibles in various nations around the world. These are humble people who have dedicated themselves to the literal, physical spreading of God's Word.

A few years ago I traveled to Slovakia, which was formerly part of the communist controlled nation called Czechoslovakia. The IBS representative assigned to that area had printed and distributed Bibles for almost forty years right under the noses of the KGB officials, and in so doing, had put himself and his family in great danger. When the Soviet Union collapsed, he was finally free to distribute Bibles without fear of being imprisoned or killed.

Two extraordinary things happened after the fall of communism. First, the government leaders of education in these communist nations found that they did not have textbooks that were free of

Soviet doctrine. The president of Slovakia asked IBS for Bibles to distribute in his nation's schools. He strongly believed his nation needed a moral foundation for the next generation and the Bible was the best book he knew to set that moral standard. He also knew that IBS could provide these books inexpensively. The IBS representative who formerly distributed Bibles in secrecy became a key person in the educational system of his nation! He had never imagined this would happen in his lifetime, but here he is, now in his seventies, having a greater influence for the spread of the Gospel than ever before.

When I met this man, whose name is Jiri Drejnar, he thanked me for my financial support. I frankly was embarrassed. All I did was write a check, which took little or no effort and involved no risk. This man had risked his entire life for the Lord and for getting out the truth of God's Word.

There's an epilogue to Jiri's story. One day before the Soviet Union collapsed, Jiri was assigned by the government to work in a hospital. Even though he was highly educated, the Soviets assigned him to a lowly job of cleaning up blood in the hospital. By coincidence—again, God's way of staying anonymous—he ended up meeting a patient who was dying of cancer. The patient recognized Jiri and seemed to know he was a Christian. He asked Jiri to tell him about Jesus and every day when Jiri went to work, this man asked to hear more. One day the patient accepted Jesus Christ as his Savior. He said a prayer similar to the one I gave you earlier in this book. And he died a few days later.

Later, Jiri discovered that this patient had once been the head of the KGB—for years he had been the one assigned to watch Jiri!

I have also met IBS workers in Africa and the Middle East who can't even have their photograph taken for fear they will be discovered. Once again, when I meet them, they thank me for supporting them. And once again, I am embarrassed for the little I do.

There is another group of people I know who are living proof to me that it isn't *how much* you give, but the fact that you are using your God-given talents and giving what you have to give, that counts. I have served on the board of a charity in Houston for twelve years. This particular charity assists children with multiple handicaps, including many who are profoundly deaf. Tragically, many of these children are born into their handicapped condition because their mothers abused crack cocaine. Some were born healthy, only to be beaten by their parents into a state of terrible disability.

During my time on the board, I have given the listeners of our radio station an opportunity to give to this charity. The radio station has raised more than a million and a half dollars for these kids. I get a lot of undeserved credit for these fundraising efforts. I am only the messenger.

The real heroes are the teachers who work with these children every day. Theirs is a tough, tough job. It can take a year just to teach some of these children how to open a door. The teachers spend years working with the children, all the while knowing that many of them will likely die before they reach the age of twenty. These teachers, however, do not give up. They don't make much money. They don't get their names in the newspaper. They don't receive awards. They just serve. I am deeply humbled by their work and dedication.

When I read about famous people giving huge sums of money to one cause or another, I am seldom impressed. I also am not impressed when a wealthy person gives money so he or she can have their name placed on a building. The Bible says, "Take heed that you do not do your charitable deeds before men, to be seen by them. Otherwise you have no reward from your Father in heaven. Therefore, when you do a charitable deed, do not sound a trumpet before you as the hypocrites do in the synagogues and in the streets, that they may have glory from men. Assuredly, I say to you, they have their reward. But when you do a charitable deed, do not let your left hand know what your right hand is doing, that your charitable deed may be in secret; and your Father who sees in secret will Himself reward you openly." (Matt. 6:1–4)

Don't get me wrong. There are wealthy people who give to the right causes for the right reasons. Without God, however, there is no *eternal* benefit to charitable giving.

No, it's not a question of your financial standing. It's whether you are standing squarely in the Kingdom of God. It is a matter of whether you are using your God-given gifts to the fullest. It's a matter of whether you are giving with a motivation of truly obeying God and seeking to benefit others, regardless of any recognition that may come back to you.

When you give for the right reasons, and to the right causes, you can't help but be humbled that God has allowed YOU to have a part in His greater work of saving souls and mending broken lives. He has allowed you through your financial giving to be in association with some of the bravest, most dedicated, and truly *good* people on this planet. He has allowed *you* to have a part in His eternal plan and purposes.

When you line up the management of your money with the principles of God's Word, you are going to be blessed in ways you can't even fathom right now. You are going to embark on one of the greatest journeys of faith you'll ever undertake, and reap some of the greatest rewards poured out to the human heart.

14

BENEFIT #8

KNOWING HOW TO TALK TO GOD THROUGH PRAYER

The Bible is the best handbook on prayer you are ever going to find.

The question about how to pray is one that is asked by many people, believers and unbelievers alike. Even the disciples of Jesus had this concern. The Bible tells us that one day Jesus was praying in a certain place. When He finished, one of His disciples said to Him, "Lord, teach us to pray." (Luke 11:1) Jesus gave these instructions about how to pray:

> When you pray, say:
> Our Father in heaven,
> Hallowed be Your name,
> Your kingdom come,
> Your will be done
> on earth as it is in heaven.
> Give us day by day our daily bread.

And forgive us our sins,

For we also forgive everyone who is indebted to us.

And do not lead us into temptation,

But deliver us from the evil one. (Luke 11:2–4)

Jesus essentially gave an OUTLINE of prayer to His disciples. He taught them that they should begin their prayer with praise. To "hallow" God's name, or to call our Father "hallowed," is to praise Him for His holiness. It is to recognize all of His infinite and wonderful traits. Too often, we begin our prayers where WE want to begin—with OUR personal needs.

Next, we are to seek God's will—the establishment of what He wants done on this earth. We are to seek to line up our lives with the way things are done in heaven, and according to what heaven desires for us to be and to do.

Next, we are to pray regularly, asking God to meet our daily needs. When we pray "give us each day our daily bread" we need to recognize that this refers to spiritual sustenance as well as physical bread. Jesus called Himself the Bread of Life. (Read what Jesus said in John 6:25–59.)

Next, we are to live in forgiveness and be generous in our forgiveness of others. This is the central theme of all Jesus' teachings. Forgive…and be forgiven. Jesus said about forgiveness:

- "If you forgive men their trespasses, your heavenly Father will also forgive you. But if you do not forgive men their trespasses, neither will your Father forgive your trespasses." (Matt. 6:14–15)

- "Forgive, and you will be forgiven." (Luke 6:37)

- "Whenever you stand praying, if you have anything against anyone, forgive him, that your Father in heaven may also forgive you your trespasses. But if you do not forgive,

neither will your Father in heaven forgive your trespasses."
(Mark 11:25–26)

- "If your brother sins against you, rebuke him; and if he repents, forgive him. And if he sins against you seven times in a day, and seven times in a day returns to you, saying, 'I repent,' you shall forgive him." (Luke 17:3–4)

Finally, Jesus taught His disciples to pray for their own protection against temptation and against all attacks from the evil one.

Jesus also taught in another part of the New Testament that our prayer life is to be, for the most part, intensely personal and private. He said:

And when you pray, you shall not be like the hypocrites. For they love to pray standing in the synagogues and on the corners of the streets, that they may be seen by men. Assuredly, I say to you, they have their reward. But you, when you pray, go into your room, and when you have shut your door, pray to your Father who is in the secret place; and your Father who sees in secret will reward you openly. (Matt. 6:5–6)

It is not in an abundance of words that God hears us. He looks on the heart. Ask the Lord sincerely and simply for what you need. Use plain English. Jesus taught:

And when you pray, do not use vain repetitions as the heathen do. For they think that they will be heard for their many words. Therefore do not be like them. For your Father knows the things you have need of before you ask Him. (Matt. 6:7–8)

Jesus also taught that we are to be bold in what we ask of God. God wants to answer our questions, resolve our doubts, meet our needs, and show us the way He has created us to live with maximum fulfillment and joy. Jesus said:

> Ask, and it will be given to you; seek, and you will find; knock, and it will be opened to you. For everyone who asks receives, and he who seeks finds, and to him who knocks it will be opened. Or what man is there among you who, if his son asks for bread, will give him a stone? Or if he asks for a fish, will he give him a serpent? If you then, being evil, know how to give good gifts to your children, how much more will your Father who is in heaven give good things to those who ask Him! (Matt. 7:7–11)

Certainly the Bible *never* promises that a person will get everything they want every time they pray. But equally true, God *always* promises us that a person who seeks Him will find Him. A person who seeks to be part of His eternal family will always be given entrance. A person who knocks on God's door of forgiveness will always have that door opened with an abundance of mercy and love. God desires to give us all the patience, wisdom, knowledge, and love we can hold in our heart and mind—and even more! He desires to fill us to the overflow point with His presence.

PRAYING IN THE NAME OF JESUS

Finally, Jesus taught His disciples to pray in His name. Consider the person who goes to a store and says, "Mike sent me." Or perhaps he calls someone and says, "Mike told me to call." If the person in the store or on the phone knows, respects, and honors

Mike, the person who uses Mike's name is doing the most effective thing he or she can do toward getting his request answered or his need met!

The same thing holds true in prayer. Jesus said, "Whatever you ask in My name, that I will do, that the Father may be glorified in the Son. If you ask anything in My name, I will do it." (John 14:13–14) The only stipulation here is that we ask those things that will bring GLORY TO THE FATHER. That's what Jesus came to do. That's what He commissions us to do "in His name."

That's the reason so many Christians conclude their prayers with, "In Jesus' name" or "In Jesus' name we pray." His name is the name that is above every other name—including the name of every problem or need we face. (I encourage you to read Ephesians 1:15–23.)

FATHER KNOWS BEST!

Let me give you a few pointers about prayer. You can take virtually any prayer request to God and expect Him to answer it. You can pray for yourself, a family member, or friends. You can pray about health matters, family relationships, financial concerns, job issues, vacation decisions, scheduling problems, and anything else you can think of!

God's answer to prayer is "yes" if what we pray is part of His will for our lives. His answer is "no" if He knows that what we are requesting will ultimately result in our harm, or if He has something BETTER in mind than what we have requested. His answer is "not now" if the timing isn't right, or if there are certain things we must do or change in order to be in the best position to receive His answer. Read through this paragraph again and you'll see that EVERY ONE of God's answers is intended for our eternal good and maximum earthly blessing.

I admit that at times I have been disappointed that God did not answer my prayers in the way I wanted Him to answer them. After a while, however, I discovered His "no" answers were always for my good. If God's answer is a certain "no," get over your disappointment as quickly as possible so you can get on to the matter of believing for what is truly God's "yes" answer!

Just because you receive a "no" or "not now" answer does not mean that God is against you. He simply desires something even BETTER for you than what you knew to pray! Do you remember the old television show from the 1950s, *Father Knows Best*? When it comes to God our heavenly Father…He truly does know what's best for us!

OUR HEART'S MOTIVATION

Underlying all prayer for others must be the "golden rule" taught by Jesus: "Whatever you want men to do to you, do also to them, for this is the Law and the Prophets." (Matt. 7:12)

There are times we don't receive the answer we seek from God because our heart's motivation isn't right.

There are other times when we don't receive what we desire immediately because God is testing our perseverance and our commitment. At times in my life I didn't receive immediately what I desired. Even so, I believed strongly what I desired was in keeping with God's commandments and God's plan for my life. So…I persisted. I kept on praying. I knew that the Lord was desiring for me to deepen my commitment, my resolve, or strengthen my faith. Jesus told a story along these lines:

> There was in a certain city a judge who did not fear God nor regard man. Now there was a widow in that city; and she came to him, saying, "Avenge me of my adversary." And he would not for a while; but afterward he said within himself, "Though I do not fear God nor regard man, yet because this widow troubles me I will avenge her, lest by her continual coming she weary me...."
>
> Hear what the unjust judge said. And shall God not avenge His own elect who cry out day and night to Him, though He bears long with them? I tell you that He will avenge them speedily. Nevertheless, when the Son of Man comes, will He really find faith on the earth? (Luke 18:2–8)

The Lord honors those who persevere in their prayers. In many ways, our own commitment to the thing about which we are praying deepens as we pray over time.

You'll also find that your heart softens and your attitude sometimes changes as you pray over time for a person. It's impossible to hate a person for whom you pray consistently and repeatedly over time. Countless people through the centuries have discovered that as they prayed for others around them to change...they themselves changed. Instead of praying for God's wrath or punishment of those who hurt you, reject you, or injure your reputation...try praying that God's will *will* be done in their lives and that God will transform their hearts. That's a prayer God always desires to answer. And in praying this way, you'll find that something wonderful happens in your life, too!

My Personal Approach to Prayer

In my personal prayer life, this is the way I pray:

I start my prayer time by saying, "Lord, first let me praise You for all the wonderful things You have done in my life and in the world." And I spend some time naming those things to God.

Then I thank the Lord for His gift of salvation, including my eternal home with Him. I thank Him for being just who He is—my loving heavenly Father, my Savior, my Lord, my ever-present Comforter and Counselor.

Next, I ask God to meet the needs I have in my life. I pray, "Lord, if it is Your will, I ask that the following things be done"…and I roll out my requests. I try to pray for the needs of others first, and then add my own needs or wants.

I always include the prayer that was prayed by a man named Jabez: "Oh, that You would bless me indeed, and enlarge my territory, that Your hand would be with me, and that You would keep me from evil, that I may not cause pain!" (1 Chron. 4:10) Jabez sought God's blessings. He sought to be used by God to take on more of the territory that was still in the hands of his enemies and God's enemies (in our case, the territory in the spirit realm still under the devil's power). He asked God's hand to be on him, guiding him and leading him in all things. And he asked that God keep him from evil's harm, and keep him from causing pain to others. What a wonderful all-encompassing prayer. The Bible says, "God granted him what he requested." (1 Chron. 4:10) I believe God answers our request, too, when we pray as Jabez prayed!

I close my prayer time by saying to the Lord, "This is what is most important to me—that You bless me so I can expand your Kingdom."

And then I end my prayer as Jesus taught, by saying, "In the name of Jesus, amen." In the next few minutes that follow my prayer, I try to listen quietly to what the Lord might speak back to my heart.

You need to pray in the manner that gives you the greatest confidence that you have communicated with God, giving Him plenty of time to speak to your heart, even as you have emptied your heart to Him. No matter the words you use, He'll hear your prayer. I have no doubt about that!

ABOVE ALL, WE ARE TO PRAY IN FAITH

The Bible makes one thing very clear. It is absolutely essential that we pray with our faith active and in full force. We must *believe* God hears us and will answer us! The Bible says, "In [Christ Jesus our Lord] we have boldness and access with confidence through faith in Him." (Eph. 3:12) The Bible also says, "Let him ask in faith, with no doubting." (James 1:6)

Many people close their prayers with the word "amen." That word literally means "may it be so." It's a statement of faith! It's a statement that conveys, "I believe that God will answer this prayer in His timing, by His methods, and for His glory. I am expecting an answer!"

That's faith. It's the key to receiving what we ask of the Lord.

BENEFIT #9

HOW TO BUILD GODLY RELATIONSHIPS AND A GODLY CAREER

I was a little surprised after I truly "put out my flag for Christ" how many people approached me to share their faith with me. I had no idea some of these people were avid readers of the Word! I wasn't particularly looking at them in that light, of course. Suddenly, after I made my commitment to serve Jesus as my Master, I discovered a number of other people around me who had also made that commitment.

Slowly, but very surely, my circle of friends has changed since I trusted Jesus to be the Master and Lord of my life.

I frankly have very little interest in being around people who are industrial-strength-size sinners. I do my best to avoid socializing or doing business with them.

As a Christian, I firmly believe that I am to live "in" the world and to be a ready witness to any person who desires to hear about Jesus or about the truth of the Bible. There is a great difference, however, in being with someone you are trying to help or who may have sought you out for a word of wisdom, and in socializing regularly or engaging in a business relationship with a person who spiritually has very little to nothing in common with you.

Remember earlier in the book we discussed the concept of oxen being yoked equally in order to pull a cart effectively? The Bible teaches, "Do not be unequally yoked together with unbelievers. For what fellowship has righteousness with lawlessness? And what communion has light with darkness? And what accord has Christ with Belial? Or what part has a believer with an unbeliever? And what agreement has the temple of God with idols? For you are the temple of the living God. As God has said: 'I will dwell in them and walk among them. I will be their God and they shall be My people.'" (2 Cor. 6:14–16)

In his letter to the church at Corinth, the apostle Paul was not saying that believers should lock themselves away from all unbelievers. He was saying that believers need to be careful not to become entwined with unbelievers. They should avoid making alliances with them or entering into vows with them. The foremost reason is that the unbeliever is far more likely to influence the believer toward evil than the believer is likely to influence a wicked person toward God. That is born out again and again in the Book of Proverbs. Our tendency as human beings is to slide toward evil. The move toward righteousness takes perseverance, diligence, and a watchful eye. It is much easier for us to give in to fleshly desires than for a person intent on evildoing to have any desire to change his ways and become more godly.

Please don't misunderstand me on this. I don't look down on anyone. I don't think I'm better than anybody else or that I'm part of a "spiritually elite" group of people. I'm just careful about the company I keep. I'm careful about the places I go. I pay more attention to the types of conversations in which I participate.

As a parent, I was very concerned when my kids were teenagers about the other teens they "hung out with" at school and in the neighborhood. I don't find it at all odd that our heavenly Father is concerned about who I hang out with now that I am an adult intent on living in obedience to His Word!

Just as my kids had a great need for a godly friend or two when they were teenagers … so I have a need today for godly friends. I need their support. I want to give them my support. It isn't easy being a follower of Christ in today's world—or likely in *any* world down through history. It's tough to go against the grain of normal human lusts and desires for power and money. It isn't easy to have a godly character. Most of the time the view of the genuine Christian—which is the viewpoint taken by the Bible—is a view that is 180 degrees opposite the world view.

What is the result when the world disagrees with you? It often is persecution. We may not face gladiators and lions today in our nation, but many Christians are persecuted nonetheless, even in the good ol' United States of America. They are shut out of conversations, kept from promotions, refused employment, dismissed from business deals, and quietly "avoided" in certain social circles. All of this is very subtle, but also very real. Persecution is often marked by rejection, being laughed at, or being ridiculed or openly criticized. Hollywood is a great example of a place where Christians have a tough time making it in their careers without ridicule.

Elsewhere, things are far more grim for many fellow Christians. There are many nations where people are imprisoned or killed for merely owning a Bible or professing that Jesus is the Savior, the Son of God.

It's at the point of persecution that we often see God's hand at work—not only in the forging of relationships in our life but also in the way *He* desires to build our career.

BIBLE BOY IN THE CORPORATE WORLD

A few years ago my family came up with a new nickname for me: Bible Boy. They mean it in good fun. They respect my new passion. They like the new me, and I must admit, their description is accurate.

I try not to wear my faith on my sleeve. In other words, I don't go around buttonholing every person I meet or turning every conversation into a preaching pulpit. I do wear a WWJD (What Would Jesus Do) bracelet on my wrist and I do have Bible-based artwork and framed verses in my office. I don't think I'm "over the top" in displaying my faith in public…but I also know this: I am more concerned with pleasing God than I am with pleasing man. I don't want to turn people off to God by my actions, but if people are offended by my bringing up the name of Jesus, so be it. I want every person I encounter to feel as if he or she can talk to me about my faith. And if they want to know where to find a Christian, I hope they'll remember they can come to me.

The Bible says, "Therefore by their fruits you will know them." (Matt. 7:20)

So how did Bible Boy get along in the corporate world?

After the Las Vegas meeting, we did sell our stations and joined a mid-sized broadcast company. We became their thirty-fifth and thirty-sixth stations. This company also owned a few television stations. That was 1995.

The company pretty much left me alone to program and manage the stations as I had always done. They were more concerned with bottom-line profits than on-air content. Our station was always one of the top performers in the company and we had the highest operating profit margin of any AM station in the nation. That gave me a lot of control and freedom as I did my job.

Over the next several years, the company experienced incredible growth as the government allowed broadcasters to own more and more stations. By the spring of 2000, the company had grown to be the largest radio company in the nation, with more than 1,200 stations. It also had become the largest owner of outdoor billboards in the world!

Sadly, as the company grew and absorbed other companies' management teams, the company's corporate culture began to change. The original owners were still in place and they were good people. However, some of the new partners they took on were not the type of people for whom I wanted to work. My new bosses, who quickly became "the management team," and I were unequally yoked.

One of the first things I was told by the new management team was that we were talking about God too much on the air. It didn't make any difference that we were still one of their top financial performers and that our format was well received as evidenced by the ratings we received. (Even with the tremendous growth of the company, we had stayed at the top of their AM stations.) The new management team simply didn't want God to be discussed on the air. I wasn't willing to change our format. It was an uncomfortable situation all around.

The new management team wasn't used to having someone buck their system. I even sent a letter to the Chairman of the Board telling him that I ultimately worked for God. Looking back, I see that was a bold statement for me to make. (I hope I did it tastefully.) I was told by an insider, however, that the Chairman didn't know what to think, much less what to do with me.

The Bible teaches that we are to respect our employers and give them an honest day's work. I always did. However, it also says that we are not to sacrifice our principles.

One day a decision was made that convinced me that I would either have to accept their way or quit. Rather than give up on my principles, I resigned. That was August of 2000. Shortly thereafter, almost all of my staff was fired or forced to resign. These were great employees who had been with me for years and I felt sad that they were replaced primarily because they were close to me.

I didn't have a job lined up when I resigned. I had been given a financial cushion from God when we sold the stations five years earlier, but I still needed to work. At age fifty, I was too young to retire.

About two weeks after I resigned, I took a long walk and had a good conversation with God. I didn't understand what had happened—at least not fully—much less *why* He had allowed it to happen. I thought I had done everything He wanted me to do with His stations.

What had I done wrong?

Why did He take these stations away from my management and programming authority?

The good news was that, regardless of the circumstances, I had learned to trust God. I had learned that what sometimes seems to be a setback is actually a lateral move so we are in a position to move forward.

The next day after my long talk with God, I got a job offer from a local independent television station. I was asked to be the general manager.

Once again, another of our nation's great pastors came into my life. His name is Joel Osteen. He pastors a church with more than twenty thousand members and he is now in the process of taking over the former home of the Houston Rockets NBA team, the Compaq Center, and turning it into what will be one of the world's largest nondenominational church buildings, seating more than twelve thousand people per service.

Like my pastor Dr. Ed Young, Joel also has a very popular national television show broadcast from his church, Lakewood Church of Houston. He is a dynamic, young pastor who took over the church after his father, John Osteen, passed away a few years ago.

Joel had become part owner of a television station and served as the general manager until his father died. At that point, Joel was called back to the church, leaving the station without a manager. His station, Channel 55, was not a Christian station, per se. It aired all the great old shows: *The Andy Griffith Show*, *I Love Lucy*, *Gomer Pyle, U.S.N.C.*, *Gunsmoke*, *Combat!*, *Perry Mason*, and others.

I wasn't sure why God wanted me to have this job, but after praying about it, I definitely felt God gave me a "green light." My main responsibility was to get the station profitable. It had been losing money since its inception. It didn't take me long to figure out that this job was not about me—it was about Joel. God wanted the burden of the station lifted from Joel's shoulders so he could focus full-time on being a preacher and pastor. It became clear to me that God wanted me to help Joel. Along the way, I also had a lot of fun hosting a nightly newscast.

Not only had I assumed that God wanted me to help Joel, but that He also wanted me to get back into television. I was wrong on that one!

What I am about to tell you still makes the hair stand up on the back of my neck. I don't remember where I heard it, but someone once told me that such a sensation is caused by "an angel moving through your life." I don't doubt it.

THE VOICE RETURNS
TO THE TEXAS AIRWAVES

In the fall of 2001 my former company had to sell one of my old stations, KSEV, the one my partners and I had purchased thirteen years earlier in Tomball, Texas. The government has a limit for the number of stations any one broadcast company can own in one city. With all of their acquisitions, my former owners were over the limit.

One of my former partners and I put in a bid to repurchase the station. I knew they would not want to sell it back to me because they wouldn't want me to compete against them. I don't say that in a boastful manner. They didn't want *any* competition. At the time I had resigned, they were so concerned that I might join another radio station that they had paid me not to work on the air for another radio station for nine months.

Nevertheless, I thought we should take a shot at the deal. We put in an offer. They had to sell by a certain date and I figured we might have a chance if no one else made an attractive offer or was able to close the deal in time. We didn't succeed in our bid ... or so I thought.

The station was sold to a group out of California that specialized in Spanish programming. I assumed they were planning to broadcast a similar format on my old station. Despite my thinking, I sent word to the new owner that I had a plan for my old station that he should consider. We set up a meeting one afternoon in late January 2001. The new owners were scheduled to take control in two months.

I laid out my plan at the meeting and told the new owner that I wasn't looking for a job. I had a great job running a television station and hosting my nightly newscast. I was looking out for my former employees who had lost their jobs, our advertisers who had lost their audience, and the audience members themselves who no longer had a format they liked available to them on Houston radio. I told him I thought he could be very profitable if he followed my plan since it had worked for twelve years.

The new owner wasn't interested in running an English-speaking talk format. It wasn't something he knew how to do. Then he shocked me. He said, "If you are so sure your plan will work, you should do it."

I wasn't sure what he meant. Then he said he would be willing to lease the time on the station to me—all 24 hours a day, 7 days a week of it. This arrangement is called an L.M.A. (local marketing agreement) in radio. I would be responsible for hiring employees, programming the station, handling all operations, and paying all expenses. I would pay him a monthly fee and whatever money was left would be ours to keep. I was stunned. He was giving me my old station back to run as I saw fit. It was the next best thing to owning it. Maybe even better than owning it!

As I have confessed repeatedly, earlier in my life I sometimes missed how God was working in my life. Not this time. It didn't take very long for me to see the incredible power and hand of God. Everything suddenly made sense. God didn't want me to be unequally yoked with my old company. God did, however, want me to continue to use the station for Kingdom building.

Almost eighteen months earlier, He had set into motion a plan to set me free from my corporate handcuffs so I could get the station back and have total independent control. In the interim He put me in a position to help Pastor Osteen.

I was struck by the awesome "arranging" power of God. My former company, now the biggest radio broadcast company in the world, could not stop God from accomplishing *His* purposes.

On my drive home from that meeting the Lord seemed to speak to my heart a new name for our old station: "The Voice."

We took Mark 10:27 as our theme verse as a station: "With men it is impossible, but not with God; for with God all things are possible!"

The Voice returned to the air in late March 2001, almost nineteen months to the day that my former company had told me to eliminate all mention of God from the airwaves.

When we returned to the air, every former employee was back on board. All of my on-air talent, my sales staff, and my office staff came back. My engineer, Chuck McLeod, and my station manager, Bonny English, who had been with me since those first days in Tomball thirteen years earlier, were back. Almost every advertiser came back immediately. And most importantly, the audience came back immediately. It was nothing short of a miracle!

Since I had signed a non-compete agreement, I could not go back on the air immediately. I could manage the station, however, until my agreement was up. In August 2001, I returned to the air. The first month, despite my having no outside advertising budget to announce our return, our ratings skyrocketed. Within ninety days, we were beating the corporate giant across the street. We were profitable the day we opened the doors.

I continued running both the radio and the television stations. It was difficult to do both. By August, I had come up with a plan to streamline the television station so it would stop losing money. I had the station's budgets in line and had done my best to take the financial burden of responsibility off Pastor Osteen's shoulders. I felt free at that point to return full-time to my radio station and I gave up television.

In the next ten months, we exceeded our three-year goal of ratings, sales, and profits. In the history of radio, there has never been a station that has become so successful so quickly. It is truly unprecedented. I know the reality of God's Word when it says:

> Blessed is the man
> Who walks not in the counsel of the ungodly,
> Nor stands in the path of sinners,
> Nor sits in the seat of the scornful;
> But his delight is in the law of the LORD,
> And in His law he meditates day and night.
> He shall be like a tree
> Planted by the rivers of water,
> That brings forth its fruit in its season,
> Whose leaf also shall not wither;
> And whatever he does shall prosper.
> (Ps. 1:1–3)

Just recently one of the key managers who had made it difficult for me to stay with my former company was "reassigned." The family that started the company is now back in charge and the new president is a Christian!

I have absolutely no doubt that great things happen to *every* person who will partner with God.

What happens in our lives is often a mystery to us at the time events are unfolding, especially if what is happening appears to be a "valley" or a time of wandering-in-a-desert, metaphorically speaking. All of us have those times occasionally—I don't know anybody who has been immune from them.

The fact is, if our lives are fully surrendered to the Lord, He is in charge of all the events in our lives—both valleys and mountain tops. His ways are *His* ways—He alone understands them. But in due course, He does reveal His plans and purposes to us. *His* plans may not be what we desire, at least initially, but *His* plans are always what will bring us the greatest amount of joy and personal fulfillment down the line. In all things, God knows best.

The Bible gives us these words of the Lord spoken by the prophet Isaiah:

> Seek the LORD while He may be found;
> Call upon Him while He is near.
> Let the wicked forsake his way,
> And the unrighteous man his thoughts;
> Let him return to the LORD,
> And He will have mercy on him;
> And to our God,
> For He will abundantly pardon.
> "For My thoughts are not your thoughts,
> Nor are your ways My ways," says the Lord.
> "For as the heavens are higher than the earth,
> So are My ways higher than your ways,
> And My thoughts than your thoughts.
> For as the rain comes down, and the snow from heaven,
> And do not return there,

But water the earth,
And make it bring forth and bud,
That it may give seed to the sower
And bread to the eater,
So shall My word be that goes forth from My mouth;
It shall not return to Me void,
But it shall accomplish what I please,
And it shall prosper in the thing for which I sent it.
For you shall go out with joy,
And be led out with peace;
The mountains and the hills
Shall break forth into singing before you,
And all the trees of the field shall clap their hands.
Instead of the thorn shall come up the cypress tree,
And instead of the brier shall come up the myrtle tree;
And it shall be to the LORD for a name,
For an everlasting sign that shall not be cut off."
(Is. 55:6–13)

Yes, indeed. If you really want to succeed in your career, give your career to God. Ask Him to help you forge only godly relationships—both in your professional life and in your personal life. Ask Him to give you the courage to stand up for what *He* says is right. Ask Him to guide you into the purposes He has for you.

You won't be disappointed. The Bible way is the best way, every time.

16

BENEFIT #10

KNOWING YOUR FUTURE— UNDERSTANDING END TIMES

Countless books have been written on the topic of the "end times"—many of them are best-sellers and a few of them have been made into popular movies. People seem deeply interested in how the world will end. It's amazing, I think, that people intuitively seem to believe the world *will* end.

The Bible addresses this issue in several books, the foremost three being Ezekiel, Daniel, and Revelation.

I'm not going to attempt to explain these books. I leave them up to your reading and interpretation. Rather, I'd like to call your attention to what Jesus had to say about the end of time as we know it, and also about *your* end time.

The Bible says that one day Jesus will return and there will be a great battle of good versus evil. When and how will we know? Those were the questions Jesus' disciples seemed to have on their minds. Jesus responded by saying:

> But of that day and hour no one knows, no, not even the angels of heaven, but My Father only. But as the days of Noah were, so also will the coming of the Son of Man be. For as in the days before the flood, they were eating and drinking, marrying and giving in marriage, until the day that Noah entered the ark, and did not know until the flood came and took them all away, so also will the coming of the Son of Man be.
>
> Then two men will be in the field; one will be taken and the other left. Two women will be grinding at the mill: one will be taken and the other left. [NOTE: This is what is known as the rapture.] Watch therefore, for you do not know what hour your Lord is coming. But know this, that if the master of the house had known what hour the thief would come, he would have watched and not allowed his house to be broken into. Therefore you also be ready, for the Son of Man is coming at an hour you do not expect Him. (Matt. 24:36–44)

The disciples also asked if there would be any signs that the Lord was returning. Jesus said:

> Take heed that no one deceives you. For many will come in My name, saying, "I am He," and will deceive many. But when you hear of wars and rumors of wars, do not be troubled; for such things must happen, but the end is not yet. For nation will rise against nation, and kingdom against kingdom. And there will be earthquakes in various places, and there will be famines and troubles. These are the beginnings of sorrows.
>
> But watch out for yourselves, for they will deliver you up to councils, and you will be beaten in the synagogues. You will

be brought before rulers and kings for My sake, for a testimony to them. And the gospel must first be preached to all the nations. But when they arrest you and deliver you up, do not worry beforehand, or premeditate what you will speak. But whatever is given you in that hour, speak that; for it is not you who speak, but the Holy Spirit. Now brother will betray brother to death, and a father his child; and children will rise up against parents and cause them to be put to death. And you will be hated by all men for My name's sake. But he who endures to the end shall be saved. (Mark 13:5–13)

A person only needs to check out today's headlines to see that there is a very real possibility that we are already experiencing the "birth pains" that Jesus spoke about in relation to His return.

I have great respect for a pastor friend of mine who has studied the Bible his entire life. He believes the world will end by 2025. For my part, I don't know. There have been many dark periods in world history when it appeared as though the end was near.

The fact is, the world may go on for several thousand more years … or end tomorrow. I surely can't predict it. Jesus said only the Father knows the precise time. Even the angels don't know—so how can any of us know.

We are called to be watchful … faithful … and ready for that day.

What I can predict with great certainty is that *you* will have an end time.

WHAT ABOUT YOUR END OF TIME?

I don't know how old you are as you read this book. I do know that within the next 125 years, barring a major scientific discovery, all six billion people on this planet who are living now will be dead. Using a simple "life expectancy chart," most people can realistically calculate the year that they know with certainty they will not be alive. Even so, you may not be here tomorrow. Everyone who died suddenly yesterday—who was in good health and under a certain age—probably didn't *expect* to die. In the final analysis, your own calculations about your own life expectancy don't mean much!

Jesus said that we are to be watchful … faithful … and ready for "our" day—our appointment with death.

So what are you going to do about your end time?

As long as you are a Christian, you don't need to be worried about dying. That will be great day for you—it is the day when you see the Lord face to face and enter into all the goodness and fullness of the eternal life Jesus Christ has promised to you.

If you haven't given your life to the Lord yet or prayed a prayer asking God for forgiveness … you are playing with dynamite and that dynamite involves your own mortality and eternal future.

THE MOMENT AFTER YOU DIE

In an earlier chapter I told you about a pastor friend of mine who doesn't particularly enjoy conducting weddings. This same pastor friend admits that he NEVER passes up an opportunity to conduct a funeral. Why? He isn't a morbid person—rather, he tells me that at funerals, people pay attention!

When a Christian dies, the funeral should be a time to rejoice! Yes, there is pain for those who are left behind and who will miss the deceased. But when it comes to the deceased who is in the near presence of God ... what a wonderful thing it is that has happened to *that* person!

When an unbeliever dies, there indeed is cause for sadness. I always feel a sadness for the person who says, "I know my friend is up there looking down on us" when, in fact, that beloved one never knew Christ. Unbelievers are clueless as to what it takes to spend eternity with God in heaven.

If I have communicated only one thing to you in this book beyond my intended goal of getting you to read the Bible for yourself, I hope I communicated to you *how* a person gets to heaven. No person gets to the "big ballpark," "ultimate golf course," "the best fishing hole," or "whatever" in the sky you may like to call heaven by being "a good person." As Mae West used to say, "Goodness has nothing to do with it."

No person earns his or her way to heaven. Apparently the vast majority of people believe in heaven. A recent *Newsweek* poll reported that seventy-six percent of Americans believe there is a heaven—seventy-one percent believe it is an actual place.

The only way to get to heaven is by believing that God sent His Son Jesus Christ to earth to die for your sins. A person has to accept Christ as their Savior, asking forgiveness for and repenting of sin. A person has to invite Jesus into his or her life.

Why am I emphasizing this?

For one reason, I don't want you to miss out on heaven.

For a second reason, that is THE POINT of the entire Bible.

I don't want you to be among those who sit in church week after week and never get THE POINT.

I certainly don't want you to be among those who never go to church and have never heard THE POINT.

The Bible says about the end of time, "There shall be weeping and gnashing of teeth." (Matt. 24:51) That will be the response of those who miss the message of the Bible.

If you know you are a Christian, I hope you will take more seriously the fact that many people you love may not have accepted Jesus as their Savior. The fact is, none of us knows the date and time of our death. Don't sit at a funeral regretting the fact that you never shared the Gospel with a loved one.

If you are not a Christian, reflect on your life and answer the question, "If you were to die in the next five minutes of a heart attack, are you absolutely one hundred percent certain that you would go to heaven?" On the basis of what decision?

The Bible says the only way to get to heaven is to believe that Jesus is the Son of God and that His death on the cross was for your salvation. When you believe in Him and accept Him as your Savior, you are born again and you receive the gift of eternal life. That's the ONLY decision that will matter to you five seconds after you die!

Every person has a free will. You can choose *not* to believe. But please, don't be one of those who "believe in God" but don't "believe God." Take Him at His Word.

King Solomon, son of King David and considered in the Bible to be the wisest man who ever lived, said, "The fear of the LORD is the beginning of knowledge, but fools despise wisdom and instruction." (Prov. 1:7)

Don't be a fool, for heaven's sake, and I mean that literally. Be wise.

GETTING STARTED

In this last and final section, I'd like to share with you a general overview of the books of the Bible, key people of the Bible, and key concepts of the Bible. At the very end is information about Bible reference books you may want to purchase as you get more and more into the Bible.

Some of this information was a mystery to me when I first started reading the Bible—I wish someone had shared with me what I'm about to share with you.

17

A Quick Overview of the Bible to Get You Started

Are you ready to dive into your Bible? I hope your answer is "Yes" or even better, "I've already started reading my Bible!"

I encourage you to make notes as you read through these pages about what you'd like to read NEXT in the Bible!

Categories of Books in the Bible

The Old Testament

The Old Testament, which some call the Hebrew Scriptures, has thirty-nine books. I have listed them in the order that they appear in Christian Bibles, and also have indicated the "type" of material that these books cover. Next to each book of the Bible you'll find the abbreviation used in this book.

THE LAW

Genesis . . . . Gen.

Exodus. . . . . Ex.

Leviticus . . . . Lev.

Numbers . . . . Num.

Deuteronomy . . . . Deut.

HISTORY

Joshua . . . . Josh.

Judges . . . . Judg.

Ruth. . . . . Ruth

1 and 2 Samuel . . . . Sam.

1 and 2 Kings . . . . Kings

1 and 2 Chronicles . . . . Chron.

Ezra . . . . Ezra

Nehemiah . . . . Neh.

Esther . . . . Esth.

POETRY

Job . . . . Job

Psalms. . . . . Ps.

Proverbs . . . . Prov.

Ecclesiastes . . . . Eccl.

Song of Solomon or Song of Songs . . . . . Song

MAJOR PROPHETS

Isaiah . . . . Is.

Jeremiah . . . . Jer.

Lamentations . . . . Lam.

Ezekiel. . . . . Ezek.

Daniel . . . . Dan.

MINOR PROPHETS

Hosea . . . . Hos.

Joel. . . . . Joel

Amos. . . . . Amos

Obadiah . . . . Obad.

Jonah. . . . . Jon.

Micah . . . . Mic.

Nahum . . . . Nah.

Habakkuk . . . . Hab.

Zephaniah. . . . . Zeph.

Haggai. . . . . Hag.

Zechariah . . . . Zech.

Malachi.. . . . . Mal.

NOTE: The Jewish or Hebrew Bible has a different order for these books, but it includes all of the above.

The New Testament

The New Testament, which some call the Christian Scriptures, has twenty-seven books. In truth, both the Old and the New Testaments comprise the Christian Bible—Christians believe in the truth of both sections of the Bible and see the many ways in which the New

Testament "fulfills" or "completes" the teachings of the Old Testament. Again, the books are listed below as they appear "in order," with an indication of the type of material in the book. The abbreviations used in this book are also provided.

THE GOSPELS

Matthew . . . . Matt.

Mark . . . . Mark

Luke . . . . Luke

John. . . . . John

HISTORY

Acts of the Apostles . . . . Acts

LETTERS BY THE APOSTLE PAUL

Romans . . . . Rom.

1 and 2 Corinthians . . . . Cor.

Galatians . . . . Gal.

Ephesians . . . . Eph.

Philippians . . . . Phil.

Colossians . . . . Col.

1 and 2 Thessalonians. . . . . Thess.

1 and 2 Timothy . . . . Tim.

Titus. . . . . Titus

Philemon. . . . . Phil.

LETTERS FROM OTHER WRITERS

Hebrews . . . . Heb.

James. . . . . James

1 and 2 Peter . . . . Pet.

1, 2, and 3 John . . . . John

Jude . . . . Jude

PROPHECY

Revelation . . . . Rev.

HIGHLIGHTS OF THE BOOKS OF THE BIBLE

Below is a very brief introduction to each book of the Bible—something of a who, what, when, and where approach—so you can jump in with some understanding.

The Old Testament

THE LAW

The first five books of the Bible are attributed to Moses, who "spoke" these books about 1450 BC to the Israelites. Over time, the very strong oral tradition of committing these words to memory became a written text. By the time of Jesus, these books were called the "Law of Moses" or just "The Law." Originally, these five books were considered to be just one BIG book. But, because scrolls could only be so long, the book was divided into five nearly-equal sections, each fitting onto one scroll.

WHERE TO FIND...

The Ten Commandments
Exodus 20:1–17

Jesus' Sermon on the Mount
Matthew 5:1–7:29

Jesus' Summary of the Law and the Prophets
Matthew 22:36–40

The Golden Rule
Matthew 7:12

The Christmas Story
Luke 1:1–2:40 and
Matthew 1:18–2:23

The Fruit of the Spirit
Galatians 5:22–23

Genesis. This book tells about creation, the sin of Adam and Eve in the Garden of Eden, the generations between Adam and Noah, the story of Noah's ark and the great flood, the generations after Noah up to Abraham, and the story of Abraham as he left Mesopotamia (Ur) and went to the place God showed him (now Israel). The book also has the stories of Isaac, Jacob, Joseph (one of the sons of Jacob), and the twelve tribes of Israel who moved to Egypt in time of famine.

Exodus. This book gives the account of how God prepared and used Moses to lead the Israelites out of Egypt and back to the "Land of Promise" that God had told them would be theirs. The Ten Commandments are found in Exodus 20:1–17.

Leviticus. This is the rulebook for the Israelite priests and people.

Numbers. This book has a number of stories about the Israelites as they traveled between Egypt and the Land of Promise—most of that time wandering in a wilderness. Various rules and rituals and feast times are described as well.

Deuteronomy. This book gives several of Moses'"speeches" to the Israelites prior to their arrival at the edge of the Land of Promise. It covers some of the laws God gave to the people, as well as descriptions of some of the "application lessons" God had given as the people wandered in the wilderness. (The Ten Commandments are also found in Deuteronomy 5:6–21.)

HISTORY

The next set of books gives the history of the Israelites as they settled into the Land of Promise, also called Canaan.

Joshua. The conquest of the Land of Promise was initially led by Joshua, who succeeded Moses in leadership. The book has a number of miracle stories and also the final words of Joshua to the Israelites.

Judges. This book describes the moral and spiritual decline of the Israelites in the years after Joshua's death. It tells how the people repeatedly sinned against God, repented and called out to God, and how God responded by giving power to a series of "judges" (ruling leaders) who delivered the Israelites from their enemies. These acts of deliverance often included powerful miracles!

Ruth. This book tells the story about a Moabite woman who followed her Israelite mother-in-law back to Judah after a great famine. It is a story about what it means to be one hundred percent sold-out to God.

1 and 2 Samuel. These books cover the life of Israel's last judge, Samuel, and the transition to leadership by kings rather than judges—first, Saul, and then, David. The books give the account of David's miraculous defeat of Goliath, David's rise to the throne, his sin with Bathsheba, the birth of Solomon, the rebellion of Absalom against David, and David's final success.

1 and 2 Kings. Originally these two books were together in one book titled "Kings." The books describe the beginning of Solomon's reign and the division of the nation after Solomon's death (into Israel, the tribes of the north, and Judah, an area to the south that included the largest tribe of Judah and the very small tribe of Benjamin adjacent to it). The Book of 1 Kings concludes with the stories associated with a number of the kings that ruled over Israel and Judah. The Book of 2 Kings tells the stories of the prophets Elijah and Elisha and gives their interaction with various kings.

1 and 2 Chronicles. These books were originally given this title in the Greek Old Testament (Septuagint): "Things Passed Over." The books repeat much of the material in 1 and 2 Samuel about the reign of David, including more details and stories about David, Solomon, the kings who ruled over the southern kingdom of Judah, the destruction of Jerusalem, and the exile of the Israelites to Babylon.

Ezra. Ezra was a scribe and priest who returned to Jerusalem in a second major wave of Israelites who were allowed to return to Judah after their years of captivity in Babylon. This book tells how the priestly functions and various religious rituals were restored, and about the return of the Israelites to a dependence upon God and governance by the Law of Moses.

Nehemiah. This book tells how Nehemiah, an Israelite who was an official in the court of Artaxerxes, was allowed to return to Jerusalem and rebuild the city's walls and gates—which prepared the way for the Israelites to return to Judah from Babylonian captivity.

Esther. This book tells the story of a young Hebrew woman who became queen of Ahaseurus (Xerxes), a Persian king. The book reinforces God's covenant relationship with His people and gives the account of their deliverance from proposed annihilation.

POETRY

This next section of books is referred to as "poetic" books although they are not written in true "poem" style with rhymes. The books, however, are rich in symbols and metaphors. They portray the "essence" of having a relationship with God, more than they give historical accounts.

Job. This may very well be the oldest *written* story in the Bible. Many believe it was written 2000-1800 BC. Nobody knows with certainty who Job may have been but this book is an excellent account of why bad things sometimes happen to good people!

Psalms. This is the songbook of the Bible. In fact, the Greek word for this book, "Psalmoi," literally means "songs to the accompaniment of stringed instruments." Almost half of the psalms are attributed to King David (73 of the 150), a few to others who were Israelite priests, one to Moses, a couple to Solomon, and several to other specific people or to "anonymous" lyric writers. Some of the songs deal with historical themes, and others address liturgical, Messiah-related, prayer, or repentance themes. You can find just about any "emotion" felt by the human heart somewhere in these songs. The vast majority of the psalms give great praise to God and extol the blessings that come to those who worship God.

Proverbs. This book is credited to Solomon, whom the Bible says wrote three thousand proverbs (1 Kings 4:32)—the Book of Proverbs only has nine hundred proverbs. At best, it is a "partial collection" of what Solomon apparently wrote. The proverbs give wisdom on a number of subjects. It is one of the most practical and easy-to-apply books in the Bible. A number of people read one chapter of this book each day of the month. (There are thirty-one chapters.)

Ecclesiastes. The word "ecclesiastes" means "preacher" and that's what this book does—it preaches about the meaninglessness of a life without respect and reverence for God.

Song of Solomon. This book is also called the Song of Songs or the "best of songs." Solomon is mentioned six times in the book so it is also called the Song of Solomon. This book tells the love story between God and the Israelites in an allegorical way. Many people also study it as a book that gives God's prescription for a godly romance and sexual relationship in marriage.

PROPHETS

This next section of books gives the teachings or utterances of a number of the prophets in Israel. A prophet was regarded as a person who spoke the *truth* of God to the people. At times what a prophet spoke was a *foretelling* of what God would do in the future, at other times what a prophet said related to a *forthtelling* of what God desired to do in the hearts of the people or the way God intended for His people to worship Him and treat one another.

Isaiah. This prophet lived about 700 BC and he gave his prophecies during the reigns of Jotham, Ahaz, and Hezekiah—kings of Judah. Many of the later chapters in the book describe the rise and ministry of the Messiah, and the ultimate "salvation" of God's people. (Other prophets who prophesied at the same time as Isaiah were Amos, Hosea, and Micah.)

Jeremiah. Jeremiah was a priest and prophet who gave most of his prophetic words during the last forty years before Jerusalem was destroyed by the Babylonians (586 BC) and the Jewish people were taken into captivity in Babylon. Jeremiah suffered intense personal persecution for his prophecies, but he continued to warn the people of God's judgment and also to offer comfort to those who trusted in God.

Lamentations. This book is traditionally ascribed to Jeremiah, and some versions of the Bible call this book "The Lamentations of Jeremiah." The book laments the destruction of Jerusalem but also has great words of hope about God's great faithfulness and mercy.

Ezekiel. Ezekiel gave his prophecies to the Israelites who were living in Babylonian captivity (in the years 593–571 BC). His message is very similar to that of Jeremiah—the sin and idolatry of the people resulted in God abandoning the Temple and allowing Jerusalem to be destroyed. Ezekiel also had a message of hope and restoration that one day the great Shepherd would regather the Israelites from the ends of the earth and establish them in their own land. Many regard Ezekiel as one of the most important books for our time today because they see it as being fulfilled in many ways with the establishment of Israel as a nation.

Daniel. This book gives the experiences of Daniel and his friends who were taken into Babylonian captivity but rose to great positions of authority and leadership as they continued to obey and trust God. The book has a number of miracle stories. It ends with the prophecies of Daniel regarding future events, including events associated with the "end times."

MINOR PROPHETS

These are the prophetic words of a number of prophets who were very prominent in their day, but whose prophecies are relatively short. The terms "major prophets" and "minor prophets" do not refer to the status of the prophets themselves, but rather, to the length of their writings. The books of the major prophets are significantly longer than those of the minor prophets.

Hosea. Hosea and Amos both prophesied in Israel (while Isaiah was prophesying to Judah). The book tells of God's love for the "backsliding" Israel—even though Israel had turned from God, God continued to pursue His people and to love them.

Joel. Joel prophesied about a severe locust plague and warned the people to turn to God in repentance. He also spoke about the "day of the Lord"—the time when the Lord would bring judgment on the whole world—and he prophesied about a time when God would send out His Spirit on all mankind, not just on selected prophets. The apostle Peter saw this prophecy as being fulfilled partially on the day of Pentecost. (See Acts 2:16.)

Amos. Amos seems to have been a shepherd and the keeper of fig trees. He gave his messages to the northern cities of Israel in the eighth century. He denounced the people for neglecting God's Word and for social injustices, self-indulgence, and idolatry. He said God's judgment would surely come. He described a series of five visions

God gave him, all of which were warnings that the people should be prepared to account for their behavior to God.

Obadiah. Obadiah predicted God's judgment on the Edomites, who were descendants of Esau (Isaac's son and Jacob's twin brother). The Edomites had plundered Jerusalem on at least four occasions. This prophecy, only one chapter long, relates to those who set themselves up to be the enemies of the Jewish people.

Jonah. This book tells the story of the prophet Jonah who was called to take a message of repentance to the enemy—specifically, the Assyrian city of Nineveh. Jonah rebelled against this, found himself in a dire situation (swallowed by a great fish that God had specially prepared), and eventually relented and went to Nineveh. He was successful in his ministry there, much to his dismay. The story is one that should inspire obedience in every person!

Micah. The prophet Micah spoke to the people of Judah during the reigns of Jotham, Ahaz, and Hezekiah. He saw the fall of Israel (the northern tribes) to the Assyrian empire and spoke about coming judgment on Judah for its social injustice. He gave his prophecies at the same time as Isaiah.

Nahum. This prophet gave his prophecies at the same time as Zechariah, Jeremiah, and Habakkuk. He predicted the fall of Nineveh, the great Assyrian capital, in 612 BC. Nahum vividly described the tyranny of the Assyrians and their downfall, and admonished the people to continue to observe their religious feasts since Jerusalem would never again be threatened by the Assyrians.

Habakkuk. This book takes the form of a dialog between God and the prophet. Habakkuk observes that the leaders in Judah are oppressing the poor and God assures him that Judah will be punished for this. Habakkuk then asks how the Chaldeans could be any better at social justice than the Israelites and God's reply is that the "just shall live by faith in God." The prophecy concludes with an assurance that the Chaldeans will in due time be judged and justice will ultimately prevail for God's people. Habakkuk closed his prophecy with a prayer of thankfulness and praise.

Zephaniah. Zephaniah warned the people of Judah and Jerusalem of God's judgment. (The Chaldeans did invade Judah from 605-586 BC.) Zephaniah called Judah to repentance and also foretold the devastation that would come to surrounding nations. The prophecy includes a promise of restoration and tells of the day when all nations would be brought to judgment and subjection to the "king of Israel," the Lord who would be reigning in Zion.

Haggai. Haggai gave his prophecies during the reign of Darius in Babylon, 520 BC. At that time, some of the Jews had returned from their exile, but little effort had been made to rebuild the Temple. Haggai aroused the people to action and the Temple was rebuilt during the years 520-516 BC. He foretold that the *glory* of the Temple they were building would be great, even though the building itself would not be impressive. He foretold a day when all nations would be "shaken" by God, with peace and prosperity ultimately prevailing.

Zechariah. This book is mostly a series of visions that Zechariah experienced. Zechariah encouraged the people to continue rebuilding the Temple and continue to obey God. He foretold a day when nations would gather for battle against Jerusalem and in the end, the Israelites would recognize Him "Whom they have pierced" and emerge in victory. Then, all nations would come to Jerusalem to worship the King, the Lord of hosts.

Malachi. This prophet spoke after the Temple was rebuilt in the second half of the fifth century BC. He was concerned with religious conditions—apostasy, intermarriage with foreigners, neglect of tithing—and spoke of God's judgment if the people continued to neglect and mistreat God. He also assured the God-fearing people of God's salvation forever.

The New Testament

GOSPELS

The first four books of the New Testament are called the Gospels. The word "gospel" literally means "good news." These are the accounts of the life and ministry of Jesus. They are like four different "portraits" of Jesus—each written from a little different perspective and to a slightly different audience. The first three Gospels—Matthew, Mark, and Luke—are called the Synoptic Gospels because they give a narrative account of many of the same events. The Gospel of John has much more symbolism in it and it appears to have been written later, perhaps to clarify or add information to the Synoptic accounts. The four Gospels need to be read as "one story" of Jesus, seeing His life as a whole while still appreciating the unique perspective of each writer.

Matthew. Matthew is "the teacher" of the Gospel writers. He was writing primarily to prove to a Jewish audience that Jesus was the Messiah. There are a number of references that show how Old Testament prophecies were fulfilled in Jesus' life. Matthew was a tax collector who became a disciple of Jesus. His account was written about 60 AD. One of the main highlights of this book is Jesus' Sermon on the Mount, which is found in chapters five through seven. The "Beatitudes" are found in the first twelve verses of Matthew 5. Jesus' summary of the two greatest commandments is found in Matthew 22:37–40.

Mark. Mark is the "story teller" of the Gospel writers. John Mark was not a disciple, but he may have been an eyewitness to many events involving Jesus. He traveled with Paul and wrote his account to the Christians in Rome around 55-65 AD. His book is very action-oriented and contains the most miracle accounts.

Luke. Luke is the "historian" of the Gospel writers. He was a physician and the only non-Jewish writer in the New Testament. Perhaps because he was a physician, Luke seems to place a special emphasis on Jesus' healing ministry and miracles that showed compassionate care of people. Luke traveled with Paul and while Paul was in prison, it appears Luke interviewed a number of people who knew Jesus personally, including Mary the mother of Jesus. As a result, some of the teachings and events of Jesus' life are only found in the Gospel of Luke. This Gospel was written around 60 AD and was aimed at a Gentile audience, primarily the Greek-speaking people throughout the Roman Empire. It is a very detailed telling of the life of Jesus. The "Christmas Story" is found in Luke 2:1–20.

John. John is considered the "theologian" among the Gospel writers. He does not chronicle the life of Jesus as much as he attempts to put Jesus' life, death, and resurrection into the greater context of God's plan and purpose for all mankind. His Gospel has many of the great "I am" statements made by Jesus. The book was probably written about 90 AD and it was written to Christians everywhere.

HISTORY

Acts of the Apostles. This book was also written by Luke, the Gospel writer. It should be considered an extension or continuation of his Gospel account. Many scholars think Luke may have planned to write a third book since Acts ends so abruptly. Luke wrote his book to the Greeks in approximately 70 AD to chronicle the beginnings of the Christian church. Again, Luke plays the role of an historian.

PAUL'S LETTERS

The letters of Paul are also called "epistles" (the Greek word for "letter"). The apostle Paul was the most prolific writer of the New

Testament. Once known as Saul, a killer of Christians, he had a powerful conversion experience and subsequently was sent by God to preach the Gospel to the Gentile (non-Jewish) world. Many of the letters are letters written as a follow-up to his personal ministry in various cities.

Romans. This letter of Paul was written about 57 AD in anticipation of a trip that Paul hoped to make to Rome. The letter is one that gives great instruction to the early church in Rome, which was composed largely of Gentiles, with a small Jewish segment. The book focuses on the theme of what it means to be in "right standing" (righteousness) with God, both theologically and practically.

1 and 2 Corinthians. These letters from Paul were to a church he established at Corinth about 50 AD. Paul lived and worked among the Corinthians for about a year and a half. He wrote the first letter a few years after he left Corinth in response to reports he had received from several sources about particular issues the Corinthians were facing. The second letter—which may actually have been two letters collated into one document—were written several months after the first letter to provide further instruction. The letters are aimed at "correcting" some misconceptions and negative situations that had arisen. The great "love chapter" is 1 Corinthians 13. In writing to the Corinthians, Paul gave very specific information about the work of the Holy Spirit in the church.

Galatians. Paul established churches in the north Galatia area of Asia Minor on his second and third missionary journeys, and he also helped build up churches in the southern Galatia area during his first missionary journey. This letter is a "summary" of the Gospel message that Paul preached, including something of an historical account and the motivation for Paul's preaching. It includes warnings not to be lured back into religious legalism, but to continue to walk and live in the Holy Spirit, manifesting the fruit of the Spirit. The fruit of the Spirit is listed in Galatians 5:22–23.

Ephesians. This letter was likely written by Paul from his prison cell in Rome (about 60 AD). Paul had taught for about two years in Ephesus and his letter to the church there was likely intended to be circulated to many churches in the area. In his letter Paul gives very practical advice about how the body of Christ is to function as the "church," how Christians are to behave in relationship to one another and to the world at large, and how Christians are to engage in "spiritual warfare."

Philippians. Paul also wrote this letter from prison (about 61 AD). It was written in part as a response to a gift that the Philippians had made for Paul's support while he was in prison. Paul had established the church at Philippi on his second missionary journey and the church was mostly composed of Gentiles. Paul gave several warnings and exhortations to the Philippians, but also expressed great love for them and appreciation for their steadfast faithfulness. This letter is filled with joy and expresses strong statements about the peace and provision that God gives to those who love and serve Him.

Colossians. Like Ephesians and Philippians, this letter was also written by Paul from prison in Rome (about 60 AD). Paul had not established the church in Colosse, but some of his close associates—probably Epaphras and Timothy—were involved in its beginnings. Paul wrote to the Colossians primarily to correct a message of "gnosticism"—a fusion of religion and philosophy that taught all matter is evil and only the spirit is good. This dangerous doctrine represented a major heresy that attempted to undermine many of the early churches.

1 and 2 Thessalonians. These letters are among the earliest ones written by Paul (about 51 AD)—they likely were written while Paul was in Corinth on his second missionary trip. Paul had established the church in Thessalonica on a three-week visit there, and Timothy was sent to teach and preach there to further build up the church. Paul wrote to the Thessalonians to correct several practical problems and misconceptions, especially ones related to the second coming of Christ.

1 and 2 Timothy. These letters are considered to be "pastoral" letters written by Paul to one of his close associates. They were written about 63-67 AD. In the first letter, Paul gave instructions related to the organization and function of the church, and also personal instructions to Timothy about how he should function as a pastoral leader. The second letter was written while Paul was in prison. It is a letter of great encouragement to Timothy to "hold fast" and continue in his ministry.

Titus. Titus was another convert and close ministry associate of Paul whom Paul left to lead the church he had established in Crete. His pastoral letter to Titus was written about 63-65 AD. By that time, Titus had worked with Paul for about fifteen years in various places. Paul gives him specific instructions about how to organize the church in Crete, outlining very specific duties and responsibilities of a pastor.

Philemon. This very short letter was written by Paul from prison in Rome. Onesimus, the slave of a man named Philemon in Colosse, had escaped from Philemon, traveled to Rome, and become a convert to Christianity there. Paul sent Onesimus back to Philemon, and in this letter, encouraged Philemon to forgive Onesimus and accept him as a Christian brother.

OTHER LETTERS

The New Testament concludes with a collection of other letters and statements, some of which have unknown authors. They provide valuable insight into the lives of those in the early church and the prevailing teachings of the apostles as the church began to grow and flourish, even under intense persecution.

Hebrews. This letter may have been written by Paul but it is in a different style than most of his other letters. The "theology" of the letter, however, is very much in keeping with what Paul taught. It was written about 70 AD and was addressed to Jewish Christians who were feeling tempted to revert to Judaism, or to make the Gospel message more "Jewish" in nature. An emphasis is placed throughout the book on Jesus being God's fulfillment of the plan He first gave to the Jews. More than twenty names and titles are used in referring to Jesus Christ. The book emphasizes Jesus' role as Priest-King and continually points toward the great salvation provided in Jesus.

James. This book may be the earliest of the New Testament letters, written about 48 AD. It was written by James, who is described in the Gospels as a brother of Jesus. (See Mark 6:3.) James was among those who were present on the Day of Pentecost described in Acts 2 and he later took over leadership of the church in Jerusalem after Peter left Jerusalem. The book points to the vital importance of coupling faith with good works, not using one as a substitute for the other. It is a very practical book that outlines the ethical nature of the Christian life.

1 and 2 Peter. These letters were likely written by Peter, one of the twelve apostles, to the churches in the northern area of Asia Minor—probably about 63-68 AD. Or, they may have been written by someone who knew and worked closely with Peter and who was very familiar with what Peter taught. Peter emphasizes the "great salvation" that Jesus Christ has provided and calls the members of the early church to have an intense and unfailing love for one another even in times of suffering and persecution. In the second letter the words "know" and "knowledge" occur repeatedly—Peter calls upon the early Christians to know with *certainty* what they believe so they can counteract false teachers and evildoers who appear to have infiltrated the church.

1, 2, and 3 John. These three short letters were written by John to encourage the first and second generations of Christian believers. The letters were written about 85-95 AD, at which time John may have been the only original apostle still alive. The first letter confronts the error of gnosticism, the second places importance on the doctrine that Jesus is God's Son in bodily form, and the third letter presents a warning to those who bring division to the church. These letters are filled with references to the love of God and they are considered by many to be the "love letters" of God to the early church. The letters were written before John's imprisonment and writing of Revelation, and before John wrote his Gospel account.

Jude. This very short letter—only twenty-five verses long—is attributed to Jude, a brother of James and a half brother of Jesus. It was written about 65-70 AD and it emphasizes the importance of "contending" for the faith, refuting error, and warning of judgment to those who turn away from obeying God's commandments.

Revelation. This book is attributed to the apostle John, written while he was imprisoned on the isle of Patmos. John was the "bishop" or spiritual leader of seven churches in the area we now know as Turkey. He was banished to Patmos for preaching about Jesus as the Christ. In some Bible versions, the book is officially titled "The Revelation of Jesus Christ Given to John." In this book, John describes a number of visions that he received from God, most of which make extensive use of metaphors and symbols. Even though most people regard this as a book about the end times, it also is a book with a strong admonition to continue to love and serve the Lord faithfully. The central figure of the book from start to finish is Jesus Christ.

NOTABLE PEOPLE IN THE BIBLE

Below is a "short list" of some of the Bible's most important figures. In all, there are more than four hundred key characters in the Bible. When you read some of their stories, you are likely to think that soap-opera scripts are dull!

The people below are listed in their general order of appearance in the Bible. I encourage you to read their stories from beginning to ending.

Key Figures in the Old Testament

Adam and Eve. The Bible states that God made mankind on the sixth day of the creation, the same day He made the animals. The second chapter of Genesis says that God formed "Adam" out of the dust of the earth. Later, God took a rib from Adam and made "Eve" from it. Together, they were responsible for ruling all of creation in the Garden of Eden. And together, the two disobeyed God by eating from the tree of knowledge, an act that God had forbidden. Their sin resulted in all mankind being born with a sin nature. After God expelled Adam and Eve from the Garden of Eden, they had three sons, Cain, Abel, and Seth. In a jealous rage, Cain killed Abel and God banished him from the family. The third son, Seth, had many sons and eventually, his descendant was Noah. The Book of Genesis says that after Seth and his son Enosh, people began talking about how man was made in the likeness of God. You can read their story in Genesis 1-5.

Noah. Noah lived in a time when the world had become extremely wicked. He was the tenth generation after Adam. God chose to save Noah and his family from a great flood that God sent upon the earth to destroy all wickedness. You can read all about the ark that Noah built, the rain that lasted forty days and nights, the worldwide flood, and the aftermath of the flood in Genesis 6–9.

Abraham and Sarah. Abraham, the father of the Jewish people and the man who is called the "friend of God" and the "father of all who have faith," was a descendant of Noah. He lived around 2200 BC. When Abram, his original name, was about seventy–five, God called him to go to a land God would show him. He traveled south through Canaan. It was through Abraham and Sarah, his wife, that a miracle child was born named Isaac. It was also through Abraham and Sarah's maid, Hagar, that a child named Ishmael was born—he became the father of many of the Arab nations. One of the most famous stories involving Abraham and Isaac was the near sacrifice of Isaac. God intervened, however, and out of that experience, God ended the former pagan practice of sacrificing children. You can read about Abraham, Sarah, and Isaac—and also Hagar, Ishmael, and Isaac's wife Rebekah—in Genesis 12–26.

Jacob. Jacob was the son of Isaac and Rebekah. He had a twin brother, Esau. Jacob fought with Esau from the time of their birth and in the end, Jacob tricked Esau into giving up his birthright and the blessing of Isaac. Jacob ran away in fear for his life and made his way to Laban, his uncle. On the way, God appeared to him in a dream that involved a ladder stretching from heaven to earth. God promised to make Jacob the father of a great nation and later, God changed his name to "Israel." Jacob married Laban's daughters Leah and Rachel, and through them and their maids, Zilpah and Bilhah, Jacob became the father of twelve sons, who became the "twelve tribes of Israel." You can read about Jacob, Esau, Laban, Leah, and Rachel in Genesis 25 and 27–36.

Joseph. Joseph was the next to the youngest of Jacob's sons. He was given dreams by God and when he shared these dreams with his brothers, they sold him into slavery. Through a series of profound and miraculous events, Joseph rose to become the prime minister of Egypt and provided for his family in a time of severe drought. You can read this wonderful story in Genesis 37 and 39–50.

Moses. Moses lived about 1400 BC. He was born in Egypt at a time when the Pharaoh had ordered all Jewish male babies to be killed. His mother set him afloat in the river, where he was found by Pharaoh's daughter and adopted by her. At the age of forty, Moses stopped an Egyptian from beating a Jewish slave, killing the Egyptian in his effort. He ran from Egypt to Midian, fearing for his life. There he worked as a shepherd for the next forty years. At the age of eighty, Moses saw a burning bush that was not consumed and God spoke to him from this bush, calling him to return to Egypt and to lead the Israelites from Egypt to the Land of Promise. As you read the story of Moses, you will encounter the plagues that God sent to Egypt, the giving of the Ten Commandments and the rest of the "Law," and many miracles of provision and protection as the Israelites wandered in the wilderness. You can read these stories in Exodus 1-20; Numbers 1, 10-14, and 20; and Deuteronomy 1–3, 9, and 34.

Joshua. Joshua was the leader of the Israelites after Moses. He had served as Moses' chief assistant for many years. The collapse of the walls of Jericho are among the miracle stories associated with Joshua. You can read about Joshua and the entrance of the Israelites into Canaan (Land of Promise) in Joshua 1–6.

Two Judges Named Gideon and Samson. Two of the most famous judges that led the Israelites in the years after Joshua were Gideon and Samson. You can read about Gideon in Judges 6–8. The story of Samson, including his relationship with Delilah, is in Judges 13–16.

Ruth. Portions of the Book of Ruth are often read at weddings. The story of Ruth is a wonderful account of faithful love and service. The Book of Ruth has only four chapters so you can read this story in a half hour or less. One of the amazing facts about Ruth's story is that she was a Moabitess and God had forbidden the Israelites from associating with the Moabite people. Ruth, however, embraced the God of Israel … and in the end, she became an ancestor of not only King David, but also Jesus!

David. David is the most famous of all the kings in Jewish history. He lived about 1000 BC. As a boy, he was a shepherd who was noted for being adept with a slingshot. He was anointed to be king by the last judge Samuel. His life story includes encounters with such colorful and dramatic figures as the giant Goliath, a faithful friend named Jonathan, the noble Abigail, the beautiful Bathsheba, and his rebellious son Absalom. You can read about David in 1 Samuel 17–27, 29–30; 2 Samuel (all chapters); and 1 Kings 1–2. Other stories about David are found in 1 and 2 Chronicles. He wrote many of the psalms and inspired or authorized the writing of many other psalms. Some people believe the Book of Psalms was David's official songbook.

Esther. The beautiful young woman Esther became a key figure in the preservation of God's people under King Xerxes of Persia. Her rise to the throne and her defense of her people against a wicked man named Haman are found in the Book of Esther 1–8.

Isaiah. Many Bible scholars consider Isaiah to be the greatest prophet of the Hebrew people after Moses. He lived about 700 BC and his prophecies involved both the foretelling of future events and strong words of admonition about current conditions in Jerusalem and Judah. He prophesied over a period of almost fifty years. He was a scholar, poet, and an intensely spiritual man. In his prophetic words, he criticized the wealthy for their lazy lifestyle and for not helping others. He also criticized those who had fallen back to idol worship. He spoke of the coming of the Messiah. Christians believe his writings foretell the coming of Jesus. As a young rabbi, Jesus referred to the prophet Isaiah and affirmed that Isaiah's prophecies spoke of Him.

Key Figures in the New Testament

Jesus. Jesus, of course, is the central figure of the entire New Testament. The Gospels are accounts of His life, teachings, and miracles. The other books of the New Testament tell how His life impacted all of history, and they elaborate practical applications of living out "His" life in the world.

John the Baptist. John was a cousin of Jesus and was born just a few months before Jesus. He became the last of the great prophets of Israel, calling the people to repentance. He told of the One who was coming who would be greater than he and who would baptize the people in the Holy Spirit. John included baptism in water as part of his preaching and thus the name "John the Baptizer" or "John the Baptist." You can read about him in Matthew 3, 11, and 14, and also Luke 1. (NOTE: John the Baptist is *not* the apostle John, who was one of the sons of a man named Zebedee. The apostle John is sometimes called John the Beloved. It is the apostle John who wrote the Gospel of John, the letters of John, and the Book of Revelation.)

Mark. He is also known as John Mark. His mother's home is thought to be a possible location for the Last Supper before Jesus' arrest and crucifixion. Mark traveled with Paul and Barnabas spreading the Gospel.

Luke. He was a physician who traveled with Paul and wrote two books of the New Testament, which comprise about one fourth of the New Testament: The Gospel of Luke, and the Book of the Acts of the Apostles.

Mary the Mother of Jesus. The angel Gabriel appeared to her one night announcing that she would bear the Son of God. Her husband was Joseph. She was also a witness to Jesus' death. You can read about her in Luke 1–2 and John 19:25–27.

The Twelve Apostles. Many people followed Jesus and adhered to His teachings—technically any person who follows Jesus in this way is His disciple, including you and me. The word "apostle" means "sent out" or "sent one" and Jesus chose twelve men from among His disciples to be apostles. They are often called, however, the "twelve disciples." They were:

- **Simon Peter**—a fisherman; he is credited with writing 1 and 2 Peter

- **James**—a fisherman and the first disciple martyred

- **John**—a fisherman who wrote the Gospel of John; 1, 2, and 3 John; and Revelation; he was the brother of the James listed above

- **Andrew**—a fisherman, brother of Simon Peter

- **Philip**—a fisherman

- **Bartholomew**

- **Matthew**—a tax collector, also called Levi; he wrote the Gospel of Matthew

- **Thomas**—known best as the one who doubted Jesus had risen from the dead

- **James**

- **Thaddaeus**

- **Simon the Zealot**

- **Judas Iscariot**—who betrayed Jesus and then committed suicide

Matthias was chosen by the casting of lots to replace Judas so that the number of apostles would remain twelve after Judas' death.

Paul. The apostle Paul, originally named Saul, was an influential and intelligent man of his time. He was once a Christian killer and an ardent skeptic that Jesus was the Christ. It was while Saul was on his way to Damascus with a death-to-Christians mandate from the high priest in Jerusalem that Saul was blinded by a bright light and heard the voice of Jesus coming from it. The Bible says, "As he journeyed he came near Damascus, and suddenly a light shone around him from heaven. Then he fell to the ground, and heard a voice saying to him, 'Saul, Saul, why are you persecuting Me?' And he said, 'Who are You, Lord?' Then the Lord said, 'I am Jesus, whom you are persecuting. It is hard for you to kick against the goads.' So he, trembling and astonished, said, 'Lord, what do You want me to do?' Then the Lord said to him, 'Arise and go into the city, and you will be told what you must do.'" (Acts 9:3–6) That experience, and his subsequent healing of blindness, left Paul one hundred percent convinced that Jesus was the resurrected Christ. He became an apostle, spreading the word of Jesus to the non-Jewish world.

(Many Christians today who have a sudden encounter with the truth of Jesus as Savior and Lord refer to their experience as a "Damascus road experience." They are likening their conversion to that of the apostle Paul.)

A BRIEF EXPLANATION OF IMPORTANT BIBLICAL CONCEPTS

Salvation

Salvation is the gift of God through grace—it is not something any person can earn. It comes by *believing* that Jesus was God's Son and that Jesus' death on the cross was the atoning, definitive sacrifice required for sin, so that all who accept Jesus as taking their place on the cross will be spared eternal death. Jesus said this to

Nicodemus, a religious leader in His day: "God so loved the world that He gave His only begotten Son, that whoever believes in Him should not perish but have everlasting life." (John 3:16) The Bible also says this of Jesus: "Nor is there salvation in any other, for there is no other name under heaven given among men by which we must be saved." (Acts 4:12)

When people speak of "being saved" they are referring to their believing in Jesus Christ as God's Son, and their acceptance that Jesus died on the cross so that they might have their sins forgiven and receive the gift of eternal life.

Grace

Grace is the favor God gives to us out of His love for us. God has every right to bring punishment upon us for our sin. Instead, out of His infinite love, He has chosen to make a way for us to receive forgiveness for our sin. We can never earn God's grace but we can *receive* His outpoured grace by accepting Jesus Christ as our Savior and then following Jesus as our Lord.

Sin

Sin began with Lucifer, who once was one of the archangels of heaven. Lucifer (also known in the Bible as Satan) sought to become higher than God. God punished Lucifer for his sin by casting him out of heaven. He now dwells on earth where he functions as the great deceiver of mankind, attempting to convince men and women to turn from God or to elevate themselves and their will above God. Lucifer tempted Eve in the Garden of Eden by enticing her to seek knowledge that would make her "like God." Adam, in turn, accepted Eve's offer of fruit from the forbidden "tree of the knowledge of good and evil" and sinned. Since that time, all men and women are born with a sin nature.

God, who is pure, perfect, and absolutely holy, cannot dwell in the presence of sin. He cannot have close fellowship with us as long as we have a sin nature. We must be forgiven of our sin before we can be fully accepted by God and enter into a full and blessed relationship with Him. God sent His Son, Jesus, to earth to die for our sins so that we might believe in Him, be forgiven, and be restored to a right relationship with God.

Redemption

To redeem something is to win back or pay the price to receive back something that has been taken away. Jesus paid the "redemption" price for mankind through His death on the cross. He paid our "sin debt" so we can have the opportunity to be put in right relationship with God the Father.

Repent

This word literally means to "turn around." It means to turn away from sin and to turn toward God. An attitude of repentance is the first step a person must take to become a Christian. Repentance is saying to oneself, "I am a sinner in need of God's forgiveness. I choose to turn away from my sin and toward Jesus Christ, who died so I might be forgiven." After we are saved, we continue to "repent" of our old sinful habits and behaviors as the Holy Spirit shows us ways in which we have not kept God's commandments or have not brought honor to the Lord. Repentance is an act of the will—it is choosing to put off old behaviors and take on new behaviors that are in keeping with God's plan and purpose for our lives.

Faith

Faith is trusting that God's Word is true and believing God will always be faithful to His Word. Every person has been given a "measure of faith." (Rom. 12:3) Our faith comes alive or active within us when we hear the truth about Jesus Christ. Our faith grows as we trust God to be true to His Word in specific situations in our lives, and then see God at work. Jesus called His disciples to grow in their faith until they had "great" faith.

Frankly, it takes faith for unbelievers not to believe in God—I call that blind faith. As believers, however, we are to have evidence for our faith. And there's so much evidence available! We have the authenticity of the Bible, we have evidence of God at work all around us and in our own lives, especially as we look back over our lives, and, we have the evidence of people who have experienced changed hearts and lives.

Free Will

God has given mankind the ability to choose between right and wrong. It is up to each individual to decide the path he or she will follow in life.

The Trinity

This concept is one that is difficult for people of other religions to understand. There is only one God. But God has chosen to express Himself as God the Father, Jesus the Son, and the Holy Spirit. The Apostles Creed, which has been a statement of faith for hundreds of years, begins: "I believe in God the Father Almighty, maker of heaven and earth; and in Jesus Christ His only Son our Lord; who was conceived by the Holy Spirit." Jesus commanded His apostles, "Go therefore and make disciples of all the nations, baptizing them in the name of the Father and of the Son and of the Holy Spirit." (Matt. 28:19) "Three in one" is the understanding of Christians from the beginning. Paul wrote, "For us there is only one God, the Father, of whom are all things, and we for Him; and one

Lord Jesus Christ, through whom are all things, and through whom we live." (1 Cor. 8:6)

The Bible says of Jesus, "In the beginning was the Word, and the Word was with God, and the Word was God. He was in the beginning with God." (John 1:1) The Bible also says, "God is Spirit, and those who worship Him must worship in spirit and truth." (John 4:24) Can a man be a father, son, and husband at the same time? Can a woman be a mother, daughter, and wife at the same time? A person is not three different people, but one. We may not be able to understand fully the concept of the Trinity, but we can believe it to be true and open ourselves up to a greater and greater understanding of God's nature as we grow in our relationship with Him.

KEY BIBLE REFERENCE BOOKS

I am one hundred percent convinced that the more you read the Bible, the more you are going to understand the Bible. The more you read and understand the Bible, the more you are going to *want* to study the Bible in greater depth. A positive cycle is created!

You likely are going to find yourself seeking answers to the questions, "What does that mean to me?" or, "Why would God have said that just that way?" You might also find yourself asking, "Are there other parts of the Bible that address this issue?" or, "Where is that in Israel?" At that point, you are ready to invest in some Bible reference books!

Concordance

A concordance is a list of key words in the Bible. Under each key word is a list of phrases that use that word and the Bible reference associated with the phrase. Many Bibles have abbreviated concordances in the back—the section may be called an index or be titled something like "where to find it." A concordance is very helpful in Bible study, especially if a person wants to read every reference related to a particular person or place, or if a person is seeking answers to a difficult problem or question. A concordance is also helpful if you remember the overall concept of a verse but can't recall where it is located in the Bible. Concordances come in various sizes— *Cruden's Concordance* is fairly small and concise; *Strong's Exhaustive Concordance Bible*, on the other hand, is fairly large and detailed!

Bible Dictionary

A number of good Bible dictionaries are available. They tell about Bible people, places, objects, customs, feasts, laws, foliage, animals, and so forth. A Bible dictionary can be fun to read, especially in explaining certain passages to a child. Most Bible dictionaries include an abundance of tables and charts—for example, tables of weights and measures used in the Bible. Most also have maps of various areas at various times in history.

Bible Commentary Books

As you study the Bible more and more, you may want to invest in books that give "commentary"—explanations and insights—on every passage of the Bible. Some of these are the size of encyclopedia sets with many volumes. They can be very detailed and in many cases, very scholarly. Other Bible-commentary books are much more devotional, with non-Biblical stories and illustrations interspersed to help give insight into particular passages. Again, explore before you purchase!

A FINAL
WORD TO YOU

At the outset of this book I told you I had two goals in mind. I wanted to inspire and encourage you to read the Bible.

And I wanted you to get the *POINT* of the Bible—which is to know the Jesus as your Savior and follow Him as your Lord.

I've done my part. Not it's your turn to act. If you haven't already given your life to the Lord, do so now. As far as reading the Bible is concerned, get with it.

Don't miss out on what God has to say to you.

Don't miss out on having a rich and meaningful relationship with God, made available through His Son, Jesus Christ.

Don't miss out on all the blessings God has for you as you follow the guidance of the Holy Spirit day by day.

Don't miss out on knowing the truth about who God is, who you are, why you are alive today, and how to live with satisfying and fulfilling purpose and relationships.

God's Word is for *your* benefit.

It is for every aspect of your life.

It is for now ... and eternity.

Will you be in heaven with me? I hope so!

NOTES